Battles

of

Napoleonic

Europe

A Solitaire Wargame

(c) Mike Lambo

2023

Books by Mike Lambo

To my constant surprise and amazement, there are now too many Mike Lambo game books to list here!

You can find my game books in hard copy on Amazon, and digital download versions on Wargame Vault (.com).

In both cases, just search 'Mike Lambo'.

If you buy through Amazon, please make sure you use your 'local' Amazon site (.com .uk .de .au .fr and so on) in order to get the best shipping rates.

Thank you for your support.   *Mike*

You can watch me play all my games on YouTube

Just search for Mike Lambo Solitaire Book Games

Follow me on Facebook (Mike Lambo)

Contents

Introduction 5

    Background 5

    How the book works 5

Rules 5

    Objective 5

    The Battle Maps (effects applicable to both the Player and the AI) 6

    The Player's Forces..7

    The Enemy's Forces..8

    The Turn Tracker...8

    The Turn Process 8

    Line of Sight rules (applicable to both the Player and the AI) 10

    Line of Sight Diagram 14

    MOVE, SQUARE and ATTACK rules (applicable to both the Player and the AI) 15

        MOVE...15

        ATTACK 15

Operating the AI 18

    The AI Chart...18

    Setting Up the AI 19

    The AI Turn – Selecting Areas..20

    The AI Turn – Activating the AI Units..21

    Examples of AI Orders 27

Setting Up a Game 31

Adjusting the Difficulty..31

Order of Play Summary 31

THE BATTLES... 31

1. The Battle of Roliça - Part 1, 17 August 1808 (British/Portuguese)...............32

2. The Battle of Roliça - Part 1, 17 August 1808 (French).............................34

3. The Battle of Roliça - Part 2, 17 August 1808 (British/Portuguese) 36

4. The Battle of Roliça - Part 2, 17 August 1808 (French).............................38

5. The Battle of Vimeiro, 21 August 1808 (British/Portuguese) 40

6. The Battle of Vimeiro, 21 August 1808 (French)....................................42

7. The Battle of Sahagun, 21 December 1808 (British) 44

8. The Battle of Sahagun, 21 December 1808 (French)..................................46

9. The Battle of Cacabelos, 3 January 1809 (British) 48

10. The Battle of Cacabelos, 3 January 1809 (French) 50

11. The Battle of Corunna, 16 January 1809 (British) 52

12. The Battle of Corunna, 16 January 1809 (French)..................................54

13. The Battle of Talavera, 28 July 1809 (British/German/Spanish)....................56

14. The Battle of Talavera, 28 July 1809 (French) 58

15. The Battle of Barrosa, 5 March 1811 (British/Portuguese/Spanish) 60

16. The Battle of Barrosa, 5 March 1811 (French).....................................62

17. The Battle of Sabugal, 3 April 1811 (British/Portuguese).........................64

18. The Battle of Sabugal, 3 April 1811 (French).....................................66

19. The Battle of Fuentes de Oñoro, 3 May 1811 (Brit/Port/Spanish) 68

20. The Battle of Fuentes de Oñoro, 3 May 1811 (French)..............................70

Suggested Counters...73

Acknowledgement

My games are based on my experiences, gained over many years, of designing my own games, but also playing games designed by others. Generally, I believe my games are different enough from those other games not to require any specific acknowledgement of any other particular game. Designers commonly borrow ideas from other games and use them to create their own games. For *Battles of Napoleonic Europe*, I did just want to acknowledge on this occasion that I was particularly inspired by the *Commands and Colors* series of games, designed by Richard Borg and published by various companies. *Battles of Napoleonic Europe* is not a copy or 'version' of those games and is in fact very significantly different, but I am sure some Players will recognise a few loosely similar concepts, and I thought it only fair to acknowledge the fact that had I never played any of those games then I would not have designed *Battles of Napoleonic Europe* in quite the same way that I have. The *Commands and Colors* games are excellent games and I recommend them whole-heartedly to anyone looking for an engaging wargame.

Introduction

Background

The Napoleonic Wars consisted of a range of conflicts, from 1804 to 1815, fought between the First French Empire under Napoleon and a changing mix of European coalitions. This game focuses on a part of the Napoleonic Wars called the Peninsular War, which took place in the Iberian Peninsula, mostly between the Spanish, Portuguese and British armies on the one hand and the First French Empire army on the other. *Battles of Napoleonic Europe* presents some of the key battles from the period. The battles in this book are representations of the actual battles they depict, but in some cases deliberate changes have been made to add to the play experience. They will, however, provide some idea of what happened at each Battle, and allow the Player to recreate, or even rewrite, that history.

In the game, the Player will be commanding various units, often representing many hundreds or thousands of men each, seeking to achieve a wide variety of Objectives. Key battles from the years 1808 to 1811 are included.

The aim of this game is to present a clear, accessible, and quick to learn game, so that players can get into the action quickly. It does not try to replace more complex wargames which often take many hours to learn and to play. It also does not pretend to be entirely realistic, and many concepts have been simplified or abstracted for gameplay purposes – it is not a simulation. Each of the 20 Battle scenarios can be played in around 30 to 50 minutes, and each one should provide plenty of replayability due to the random set up of the initial forces and depending on how the Battle plays out.

Thank you for purchasing the book and I hope you enjoy the challenges it presents!

How the game works

This game is a solitaire wargame. You play the game, and the enemy is controlled by the game book (or the Artificial Intelligence or 'AI'). You will need a good handful of standard six-sided dice to play (ten should be sufficient). Methods to play the game include:

- Remove or copy the counters provided on the final page of the book, stick them to card and cut them out. These are also available on BoardGameGeek.com in the Files section for the game.
- Photocopy the maps and draw/write on the pages lightly in pencil and erase when necessary. You can use any annotations you choose for the units, that make sense to you.
- Lay the book flat (it's well-bound, it can stand it!) and use cubes, miniatures, or similar tokens for the units.
- Use some kind of acetate and dry-wipe markers.
- Take a photo of the maps on a tablet and use the "edit" function to draw and erase. For example, on an iPad, tap "edit" in the Photos App and then tap the three dots in the circle and choose 'mark-up'.

Rules

Objective

Each Battle will provide an Objective which must be completed in order to deem the Battle a success. For example, Battles may require you to occupy a particular hex, destroy the enemy entirely or prevent the enemy from doing something before the Turn Tracker runs out. Victory is achieved if the Objective is achieved. Always take careful note of the Objective – you cannot succeed without it! Note that eliminating the other side entirely is *always* deemed to be an immediate victory for the remaining army, regardless of any other Objective or condition stated in the Battle's description.

The Battle Maps (effects applicable to both the Player and the AI)

Each Battle Map consists of a series of hexes on which your units, and the enemy units, will be placed and move. Some hexes have terrain features such as trees and high ground. These features look like, and have the effect noted in, the chart below. When performing Attacks (explained in full later) the attacker rolls a number of dice. The more dice rolled, the more likely that an attack will be successful. Terrain can affect the number of dice rolled, and so is an important tactical consideration.

Terrain Feature	Graphic	Effect
Trees		Attacking *into*, or *through* Trees results in the **removal of 1 die** for each such occasion. Trees do *not* block Line of Sight.
Buildings		Attacking *into* Buildings results in the **removal of 1 die** for each such occasion. Buildings block Line of Sight through them (but not *into* them).
High Ground		Attacking *from* Higher Ground results in the **addition of 1 die** if the target is on lower ground. High Ground can block Line of Sight and also allows units to see 'over' other units (explained later).
Clear (no terrain)		None.
River or Stream		Attacking *from* a River/Stream results in the **removal of 1 die**. These Rivers/Streams can be crossed at all points.
Sea or Estuary		No unit can enter these hexes.

There are also numbers at the top and bottom of the Map in blue and red circles. These numbers represent an Area of the Map, with each Area consisting of the two complete vertical columns (up and down the Map) adjacent to the number.

Area 1 consists of the two left most columns.
Area 2 consists of the third and fourth columns.
Area 3 consists of the fifth and sixth columns (the two central columns).
Area 4 consists of the seventh and eighth columns.
Area 5 consists of the two right most columns.

Red dotted lines have been added here to help highlight the five different areas. These will not appear on the actual Battle Maps. Note that each Area is numbered the same for both the Player and the AI.

The Player's Forces

The Player will have control of the armies on one 'side' of each Battle and the armies will consist of various units. Details of the relevant units can be found in the Player Chart on the page adjacent to each Battle Map. That chart will look like this:

Player: British & Portuguese		Place each Unit below the red dashed line	
Infantry: 5	Cavalry: 2	Artillery: 1	Commander: Sir Arthur Wellesley
Roll 3 dice. **Re-roll any dice once** (all together). **If Commander not KIA**, then 6s are Wild			

In this example, the Player controls the British and Portuguese army and starts the Battle with five Infantry units, two Cavalry units, one Artillery unit and a Commander. The other information in this Chart will be covered later. More information on the units can be found in the Unit Statistics Chart, which is the same for every Battle, applies to units on *both* armies, and looks like this:

Unit	M	R	Units cannot Move if Square/engaged in battle	v Inf	v Cav	v Art
Infantry	1	3	Move or Square/De-Square, then Attack	4 - 3 - 2	3 - 2 - 2	3 - 2 - 2
Cavalry	2	1	Move, then Attack	6 - 5 - 4	4 - 3 - 2	4 - 3 - 2
Artillery	1	6	Move or Attack	3 - 2	2 - 1	2 - 1

The Move (M) statistic determines how many hexes a unit can Move on its Activation. As can be seen, all units Move one hex at a time, except Cavalry which can Move up to two hexes. Note that the Commander is deemed to be a Cavalry unit for all purposes. The Range (R) dictates how far a unit can Attack. Cavalry units can only Attack an enemy unit which is located in one of the six hexes adjacent to it, because their Range is one hex. Infantry, on the other hand, can Attack units which are either one, two or three hexes away from them. Artillery have a Range of six hexes (although exactly how they operate is covered later). In order to Attack an enemy unit, the attacking unit needs to have that enemy unit in its Range and also in its Line of Sight, which will be explained later.

Finally, the chart shows the number of dice rolled by each particular unit when attacking an enemy unit. **Infantry** and **Cavalry** units always start Battles with a **strength of three** and as they are successfully attacked, their strength reduces to two and then to one and finally to zero when they are defeated and removed from the game. **Artillery** units always start battles with a **strength of two** and as they are successfully attacked, their strength reduces to one and finally to zero when they are defeated and removed from the game. **Commanders** always have a **strength of one** and, as stated earlier, are treated as Cavalry units for the purpose of Movement and Attacking. One successful Attack against them, however, is enough to remove them from the game. It can be seen from the above chart that the number of dice rolled reduces as units lose their strength. The numbers of dice in the chart are positioned in a way that represents the strength of the attacking unit. In each box, the first number relates to a full strength unit, and subsequent numbers relate to a reduced strength unit. The *strength* of the *target unit being attacked* is not relevant.

For example, the chart shows that a full strength Infantry unit (with a strength of three) will roll four dice when attacking an enemy Infantry unit (the first number shown in the Infantry v Infantry box). When its strength reduces to two, it will roll three dice against enemy Infantry units, and when its strength is reduced to one it will roll two dice against enemy Infantry units.

As another example, a full strength Artillery unit (strength two) will roll two dice when attacking an enemy Cavalry unit, but once an Artillery unit is reduced to strength one it will only roll one die against an enemy Cavalry unit. Commanders always Attack as strength one Cavalry units.

The number of dice rolled may be modified by Terrain features (see above) and other factors explained later in these Rules.

Note that the basic number of dice rolled initially depends on the *type* of unit being targeted. Cavalry, for example, are very effective against Infantry units.

The Enemy's Forces

The enemy is controlled by the game (or the Artificial Intelligence or 'AI') which uses the same types of units and the same game rules as the Player. Enemies are placed at the start of the game as explained in 'Setting Up the AI' below and, as with the Player's forces, all start with full strength. They will then Move and Attack just like a real player might, in accordance with their instructions, which are discussed later, under 'Operating the AI'.

The Turn Tracker

Beneath the map is the Turn Tracker. Mark, or place a counter of some kind in the first turn box (numbered "1") and move it along the boxes as you proceed through the turns. Mark the relevant Turn before playing that Turn; it is the first thing to do on each Turn. Once the final section of the Turn Tracker is marked and that Turn is subsequently completed, the Battle comes to an end. If that stage is reached, then assess whether the Objective has been achieved or not to determine whether a victory has been achieved. If you do not win, you lose – there are no draws here!

The Turn Process

The game proceeds through each turn as follows:

1. Mark off the next section of the **Turn Tracker** to signify that a new turn is beginning.

2. The **Player takes their Turn** by undertaking the following steps in order:

A) **Roll three dice** to determine the Areas in which they can activate units this Turn. The Player *may* (but does not have to) choose to **re-roll** any number of dice *once only*. Note that if the Player elects to re-roll more than one die, they *must* be re-rolled together. The re-rolled results must be kept (the original dice results are replaced).

The Commander Ability (Player)

 Once any dice have been re-rolled, if the Player's Commander is still in play (has not been killed) then any **6s** rolled by the Player are classed as '**wild**' and the Player may change them to show any result not otherwise rolled on another die.

Example: If the Player rolls 3,3,6 then they will certainly want to re-roll one of the 3s (and may decide to re-roll both, depending on whether they have units in Area 3 that they want to Activate this Turn or not). If they re-roll a 3 and it shows a 6, then the final dice results will be 3,6,6. The Player can then change the two 6s to show a 1,2,4 or 5 (each one showing a different number). Any 6s rolled after the Commander has been killed are redundant (they cannot be changed and there is no Area 6) and so should always be re-rolled to try to obtain a 1-5 result.

B) Place each die on its matching 'Area' number at the *bottom* of the page (the Player end). *Any duplicate dice and 'unchanged' 6s are discarded.* The Player will be able to Activate (once), in this Turn, all of their units which are currently positioned anywhere in either of the two Columns of hexes making up each of the Areas into which a die has been placed.

Example: The Player rolls 2,4,5 but desperately wants to Activate units in Area 1. They decide to re-roll the 2 and the 4 again, because Area 5 also has units in it which the Player wants to Activate. The final dice results rolled are 1,5,5. Whilst the Player can now successfully Activate their units in Areas 1 and 5, the *duplicate* 5 is wasted and must be discarded - units in each Area can only be Activated once per Turn.

C) Once the dice are finalised, select each Area which has a die allocated to it in turn (in any order) and Activate each unit in that Area one by one (in any order) until they have all Activated. Then select the next Area and so on. Each unit can Move, go into and out of Square formation (Infantry only) and/or Attack as desired and as permitted by the Units Chart on the page adjacent to each Battle Map. Each unit can only be Activated once, even if it Moves into another Area which also has a die allocated to it. When this happens, it is useful to mark such units temporarily so that they are not mistakenly Activated twice. Of course, the Player can always opt *not* to perform any Order with a particular unit. The Chart looks like this, you will recall:

Unit	M	R	Units cannot Move if Square/engaged in battle	v Inf	v Cav	v Art
Infantry	1	3	Move or Square/De-Square, then Attack	4 - 3 - 2	3 - 2 - 2	3 - 2 - 2
Cavalry	2	1	Move, then Attack	6 - 5 - 4	4 - 3 - 2	4 - 3 - 2
Artillery	1	6	Move or Attack	3 - 2	2 - 1	2 - 1

Infantry can either Move <u>or</u> go into a Square formation (or come out of Square formation) and *then* Attack. They *cannot* Move when in Square formation, including on the same Activation as they come out of Square formation. To be clear, an Infantry unit can therefore do one of the following:

➢ *Move (when not in Square formation), then Attack*
➢ *Form a Square, then Attack*
➢ *Come out of Square formation (De-Square), then Attack*
➢ *Perform any <u>one</u> of the above Orders (Move, Square, De-Square, Attack)*
➢ *Do nothing*

 Cavalry can *Move (one or two hexes) then Attack, or just Move (one or two hexes), or just Attack, or do nothing.*

 The **Commander** is a *Strength one* Cavalry unit and so *has the same options as Cavalry units.*

 Artillery can either *Move or Attack, but not both, or do nothing.*

3. The **AI then takes its Turn**, during which it will select the Areas in which it will Activate units and then Activate those units in accordance with its own procedure and instructions set out below under 'Operating the AI'.

Example of Player Area Selection and Unit Activation

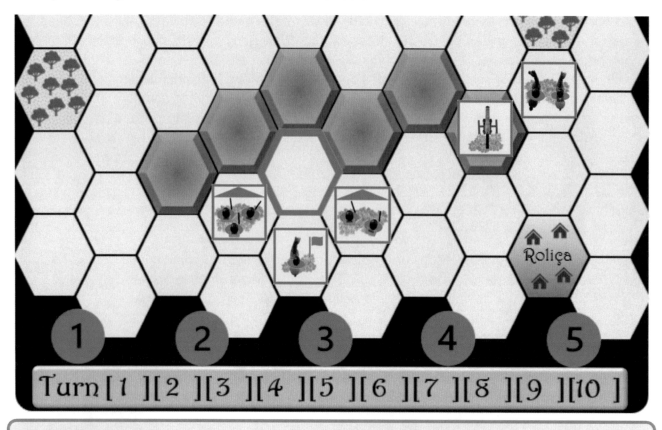

On their Turn, the Player rolls three dice which we will assume show 1,4,4. The 1 is no use to the Player as they have no units in Area 1. One of the 4s might be useful if the Player wants to Activate their Artillery unit. The second 4 is redundant as the units in each Area can only be Activated once per Turn. The Player decides that they *do* want to Activate their Artillery and so chooses to re-roll the 1 and the second 4, which now show 3 and 6. The 3 must be allocated to Area 3 (although the Player could choose not to perform any Orders with the units in that Area). The 6 is Wild, because the Player's Commander is still in play, and can be allocated to Area 1,2 or 5. The Player is likely to select Area 2 or 5 of course, and the choice will depend on whether they want to Activate their Strength 3 Infantry or their Strength 2 Cavalry. Note that if the Player's Commander had already been killed in this Battle, then the 6 would be redundant as the Commander Ability (to change 6s into other numbers) would have been lost.

Line of Sight rules (applicable to both the Player and the AI)

In order to be able to Attack another unit, the Attacking unit must be able to *see* its target. Line of Sight can be blocked by Buildings hexes, Higher Ground and other units, both friendly and enemy:

❖ **Buildings** hexes block Line of Sight *through* them (unless *both* the Attacking unit *and* target unit are on Higher Ground, in which case the Attack goes 'over' the intervening Buildings). A particular Buildings hex does not block Line of Sight into or out of itself.

❖ **Higher Ground** hexes block Line of Sight *through* them unless *both* the Attacking unit and target unit are themselves on Higher Ground, in which case intervening Higher Ground hexes do *not* block Line of Sight. A particular Higher Ground hex does not block Line of Sight into or out of itself. Higher Ground hexes do *not* enable units on them to see 'over' Trees hexes (thus avoiding the Tree hex penalty) or Buildings hexes, unless their target is *also* on Higher Ground. Higher Ground is higher, but not so high that it provides that kind of view. However, Higher Ground does allow a unit to see over other *units*. Remember, people are smaller than Trees and Buildings!

Lines of Sight examples for Higher Ground The Green arrows indicate a clear Line of Sight. The Orange arrows indicate Lines of Sight where a penalty to Attack will apply due to the Trees. The Grey arrow indicates a Line of Sight which gives both a Trees and Buildings penalty to Attack. The unit next to the red cross cannot be seen due to the Buildings.

❖ **All units** block Line of Sight *through* the hex they occupy (unless <u>*either or both*</u> of the Attacking unit and target unit are on Higher Ground, in which case the Attack goes 'over' the intervening unit(s) – see the examples above).

In the case of **Cavalry** units, because they only attack into *adjacent* hexes, Line of Sight is not an issue for them. All units can *always* see into *every* adjacent hex.

Artillery units only Attack along *straight lines* of hexes (see '**ATTACK**' below) and therefore establishing Line of Sight is reasonably straightforward. Once the line of hexes they are Attacking along has been chosen (by the Player or AI) then the Artillery unit can only Attack enemy units along that line of hexes to which the Artillery unit has Line of Sight.

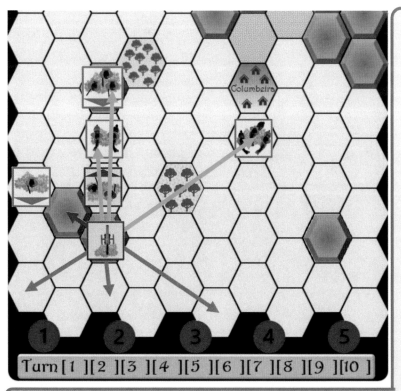

The British Artillery attacks along any of the **six** lines of hexes running from its own hex. It can therefore potentially Attack all the enemy units on this example Map.

It has Line of Sight to the three strength Cavalry unit because Tree hexes do not block Line of Sight.

It does **not** have Line of Sight to the one strength Infantry unit because the intervening Higher Ground hex blocks it (often referred to as the 'plateau effect').

It has Line of Sight to the two strength Cavalry unit because it can see over the British Infantry unit (that potentially blocks Line

of sight) because the Artillery is on Higher Ground.

It also has Line of Sight to the three strength Infantry unit because both units are on Higher ground and therefore it can again see over the intervening units.

As a side note, if the Artillery Attacked the three strength Cavalry, it would still suffer a penalty for Attacking through a Trees hex. Higher Ground is higher, but it is not so high that it provides that kind of clear view of the terrain beyond. If the Trees hex was a Buildings hex, then that would still block Line of Sight to the Cavalry. The Tree hex (and any Buildings hex) would, of course, be ignored if the target Cavalry were themselves also on Higher Ground.

Infantry units which Attack an enemy unit in an adjacent hex are deemed to be attacking in melee combat. As with other units, Line of Sight is not an issue when doing this as units can *always* see into *all* adjacent hexes. When infantry units attack an enemy unit which is two or three hexes away, Line of Sight is a little more complex but still follows the basic rules. As explained in the **ATTACK** section below, infantry units controlled by the Player will only ever face upwards and infantry units controlled by the AI will only ever face downwards, and in both cases, when they attack at Range 2 or 3 they can only see and attack the hexes which are in their front arc of fire.

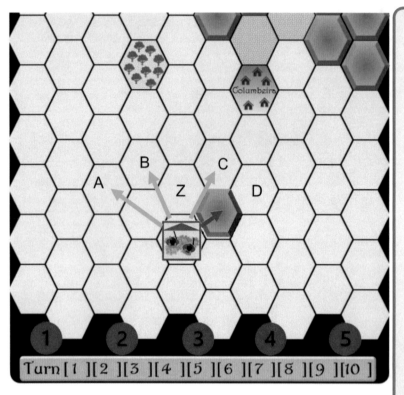

When considering the Line of Sight of an Infantry unit, an imaginary line is drawn from the centre of its own hex to the centre of the hex it is targeting. Before you reach for the string or laser, please be assured that these are not required! If targeting a hex two hexes away, the target hex will either be in a direct line of hexes with the Attacking unit and Line of Sight will travel *through* just one hex (see example A) or it will be directly behind two hexes and Line of Sight will travel between those two hexes (see example B).

In case A, the usual Line of Sight rules apply in the same way as they did for Artillery above. For example, the Infantry unit cannot see hex D (which is the same as case A) because the Higher Ground blocks Line of Sight.

In case B, Line of Sight is only blocked if *both* hexes are 'blocking' hexes – for example, if both contained units. If one hex is blocked and the other is a Trees hex, then Line of Sight exists through the Trees hex and the usual 'through a Trees hex' penalty is applied for such an Attack. As ever, if the Attacker and the target are *both* on Higher Ground, then any potentially blocking unit on lower ground, Buildings hex or Higher Ground hex between them will be ignored, as would the penalty effect of any Trees hex.

The Infantry unit above can see hex C (which is the same as case B) because *one* of the intervening hexes (Z) is clear. If Z had a unit in it, or was a Higher Ground or Buildings hex, then the Infantry unit would not be able to see hex C. If Z was a Trees hex, the Infantry unit would still be able to see hex C but it would suffer a penalty to its Attack for Attacking through Trees. *For clarity, if hex Z was a Trees hex and the Higher Ground hex was a standard clear hex, then the Attack would not suffer the Trees hex penalty.* Basically, in cases B and C above, the Attacking unit is deemed to be Attacking through the ***most advantageous of the two intervening hexes***.

When Infantry Attack a unit which is three hexes away, there will always be *two* intervening hexes and Line of Sight will always travel through *both* of those two hexes. The diagram below exemplifies this.

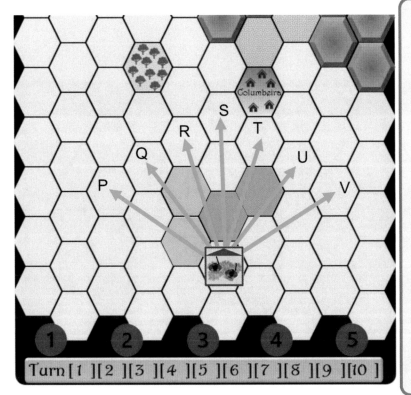

Cases P, S and V are easy and the usual Line of Sight rules apply as they did for Artillery, and in Case A earlier when we looked at Infantry Attacking a unit two hexes away.

For cases Q, R, T and U, the Player needs to assess the situation in the two directly intervening hexes between the Attacker's hex and the target unit's hex. The two relevant intervening hexes through which the Line of Sight travels are the two hexes through which the imaginary line would pass, running from centre of Attacker's hex to centre of the target's hex. These have been shaded in orange for case Q and purple for case T for clarity.

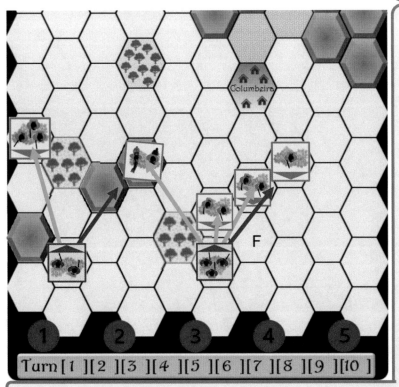

The two strength British Infantry unit has Line of Sight to the Three strength French Infantry unit because both of the two directly intervening hexes are clear. The Trees hex is not in the path of the Line of Sight and therefore no penalty is applied.

The two strength British Infantry unit does **not** have Line of Sight to the two-strength French Cavalry because it is blocked by the intervening Higher Ground, and the British unit is not itself on Higher Ground.

The three strength British Infantry unit has Line of Sight to the two

strength French Cavalry unit but it will suffer a penalty for Attacking through the Trees hex – the Higher Ground does not negate this. It does **not** have Line of sight to the one strength Infantry unit because the second (furthest up) French two strength Infantry unit is blocking it. It does have Line of Sight to both of the French two strength Infantry. In relation to the second (furthest up) unit, Line of Sight would only be blocked if hex F blocked Line of Sight or contained a unit.

Line of Sight Diagram

This diagram provides numerous common examples of Line of Sight to help Players. Green arrows show clear Lines of Sight and red arrows show blocked Lines of Sight, with red labels on the feature or unit that blocks it. Relevant dice adjustments (for Trees) are also shown as labels. All Lines of Sight are reciprocal.

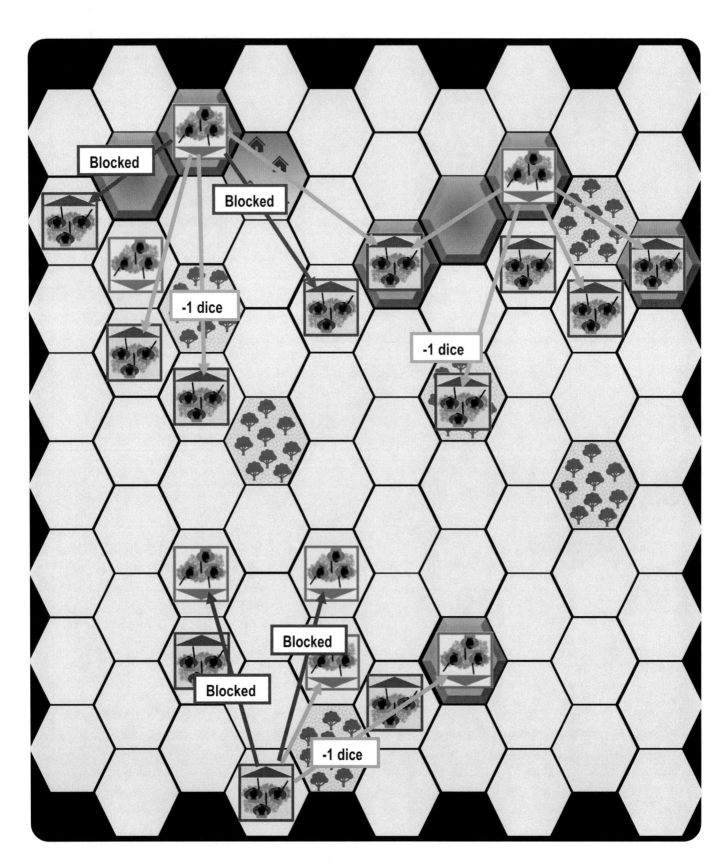

MOVE, SQUARE and ATTACK rules (applicable to both the Player and the AI)

MOVE

Infantry and Artillery units can Move one hex in any direction. Cavalry (including the Commander) can Move one or two hexes in any direction. Each hex can only have one unit in it at any time (friendly or enemy). Units cannot therefore pass through each other (friendly or enemy).

River hexes can be entered (but note that a unit in a River hex suffers an attack penalty – see below).

Units cannot Move if they are adjacent to *any* enemy unit (but they do still **retreat** when Attacked – see below), and a Cavalry unit *must* therefore stop if it Moves adjacent to an enemy unit on its first Move. Such units are deemed to be 'engaged in battle' and therefore "stuck" until all adjacent enemy units have been destroyed, or retreat. (Units engaged in battle *cannot* Attack units with which they are not engaged – see below). A unit can be engaged in battle with more than one enemy unit at a time.

ATTACK

Cavalry (including the Commander) and **Infantry** units can Attack *one* enemy unit within Range. Cavalry units have a Range of one and can therefore only Attack *adjacent* enemy units. Infantry units have a Range of three and can Attack enemy units within three hexes.

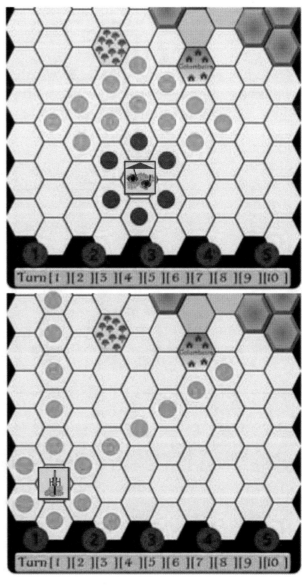

When Attacking at a Range of two or three hexes, **Infantry** units can only see and therefore Attack units in their *front arc of fire* (shown by the blue circles in the diagram to the right). Infantry units are deemed to always be facing up (or, for the AI, down) the Map. If using the counters at the back of the book, the Infantry units have arrows on them to remind the Player of this. Due to the formations of Infantry units, turning was problematic, especially in the heat of battle. Therefore, the scope for Attacking to the 'side' is limited in this game. This can allow Cavalry units to flank enemy Infantry when the chance arises. When Attacking at a Range of one hex (in Melee) Infantry units can Attack in *any* direction (**red circles**), as can Cavalry, of course.

Artillery can only Attack along *straight lines* of hexes, emanating from their current hex, in *any* of the six directions (shown by the blue circles in the diagram to the right). Their Range is six hexes. The Player or AI can select any one of the six directions to Attack along, but of course they must always target an enemy unit which is in Line of Sight along the chosen line of hexes.

Units which are engaged in battle can only Attack the unit (or *one* of the units) with which they are engaged, and they *can* be Attacked by other units which are not engaged with them.

To perform any Attack by any unit, the appropriate number of dice are rolled as per the Unit Statistics Chart referred to earlier, which you will recall looks like this:

Unit	M	R	Units cannot Move if Square/engaged in battle	v Inf	v Cav	v Art
Infantry	1	3	Move or Square/De-Square, then Attack	4 - 3 - 2	3 - 2 - 2	3 - 2 - 2
Cavalry	2	1	Move, then Attack	6 - 5 - 4	4 - 3 - 2	4 - 3 - 2
Artillery	1	6	Move or Attack	3 - 2	2 - 1	2 - 1

As an example and a reminder, an Attack by a strength two Cavalry unit on an enemy Artillery unit would result in three dice being rolled (as highlighted in the chart above for clarity).

Before rolling, carefully note the modifiers that apply to this value based on the Situation or Terrain Chart found on the page adjacent to each Battle Map which summarises the relevant information from these rules. Some of the information in that chart has already been explained, and some it will be explained below (the rest of it is self-explanatory). Here is the full chart for reference – it is the same for every Battle:

For example, if the Artillery unit in the above example was in a Trees hex, then the Attacking Cavalry unit would only roll two dice instead of three, as the chart states that one die is deducted when any unit is Attacking a unit on a Trees hex. If the number of dice falls below one then no dice are rolled

Situation or Terrain (Units, High Ground & Buildings block LoS)	Dice
Infantry attacking *at Range 1* after Moving	+1
Infantry attacking *at Range 2-3* after Moving	-1
Infantry attacking *at Range 2-3* whilst in Square formation	-1
Infantry attacking Infantry who are in Square formation	+1
Cavalry attacking Infantry who are in Square formation	-3
Artillery attacking at Range 1-3	+2
Artillery attacking Infantry who are in Square formation	+2
Any unit attacking which is adjacent to its Commander	+1
Any unit attacking from Higher Ground than its Target	+1
Any unit attacking a unit in Trees or Buildings	-1
Any unit attacking through intervening Trees	-1
Any unit attacking from a River hex	-1

and the Attack does not take place.

Performing the Attack
The Player rolls the appropriate number of dice:
- All **1s, 2s and 3s** are **misses** and are disregarded.
- Every **5 and 6** are **hits** which reduce the target unit's strength by one for each hit. If its strength falls to zero it is removed from the game.
- Every **4** causes the target unit to **Retreat** by one hex **except:**
  - Commanders, who never Retreat – in that case ignore any 4s rolled.
  - Infantry units in Square formation which never Retreat – in that case ignore any 4s rolled.
  - Any unit adjacent to its Commander *when the Attack is performed* – again ignore any 4s rolled.

Retreats are performed *after* any hits are applied. Units do not become engaged in battle as they Retreat (unless they finish their full Retreat adjacent to an enemy unit of course). **For each Retreat: First**, the unit must try to Retreat **directly back** towards its own 'end' of the Map, along the column of hexes in which it is currently positioned. **Second**, only if that hex is blocked by other units (friendly or enemy), or by a 'Sea or Estuary' hex, or is off the Map, then the unit will try to Retreat back towards its own 'end' but into an adjacent column. In this case, the Player (and the AI, using the TB1 table explained later) can select which of the two hexes it will Retreat to if there is a choice. If it cannot Retreat, because its way is blocked entirely (by units or an impassable water hex for example), then it loses one strength point for each Retreat it is unable to perform. Units engaged in battle *can* and must Retreat if possible.

Examples of units retreating

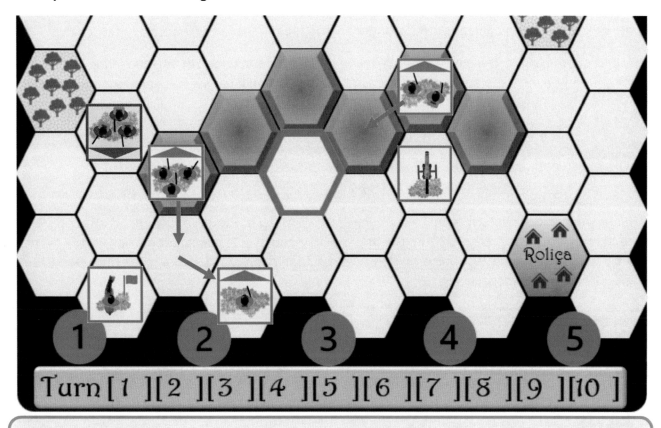

(1) Assuming the French three-strength Infantry unit is Attacked and the dice show one hit and three 4s, then it loses one strength to become a two-strength unit and then must retreat three hexes, even though it is engaged in battle. It *must* first try to retreat directly back towards its own 'end' and so it will retreat directly back into the hex below it. Its second retreat would take it off the Map but it can still retreat to one of the two hexes which are in the two adjacent columns and which are still *back* towards its own 'end'. It has to retreat to the right due to the other hex being occupied. Note that because the Infantry unit was not adjacent to its Commander *when the Attack was performed,* the presence of the Commander does not stop the retreat once it has started. The unit's third retreat would again be off the Map but this time *any* retreat would be off the Map and so the unit instead loses one strength point and becomes a one-strength Infantry unit.

(2) Assuming the French two-strength Infantry unit is Attacked and the dice show no hits and one 4, then it must try to retreat directly back. As its path is blocked by its own Artillery unit, the Player must choose between the two High Ground hexes behind it in the two adjacent columns. In this case the Player decides to retreat the unit towards the blue Objective hex.

SQUARE

Infantry units (only) can go into Square formation (literally form a Square). Historically, this allowed them to fend off attacks from highly mobile enemy Cavalry units more effectively than when they were in standard formation which tended to be a long thin line. However, it made them less effective when making Ranged Attacks and more vulnerable to enemy Infantry and Artillery fire, because the men were more packed together. The 'Square' action also includes *coming out* of Square formation (back into line formation). Infantry units in Square formation should be marked in some way to indicate this.

Units in Square formation **cannot** Move and they will **never** retreat, so any 4s rolled against them in Attacks are ignored. Units which are engaged in battle **cannot** change formation so must remain in Square or line formation until they are no longer so engaged. Units in Square **can** Attack.

As well as not retreating, the other effects of being in Square formation can be seen in the Terrain or Situation Chart on the page adjacent to each Battle Map. The relevant sections are reproduced here:

Situation or Terrain (Units, High Ground & Buildings block LoS)	Dice
Infantry attacking *at Range 2-3* **whilst in Square formation**	-1
Infantry attacking Infantry **who are in Square formation**	+1
Cavalry attacking Infantry **who are in Square formation**	-3
Artillery attacking Infantry **who are in Square formation**	+2

An Infantry unit in Square formation loses 1 die when Attacking at Range 2-3 (so not if Attacking in Melee at Range 1). The protection from Cavalry is evidenced by a significant reduction in dice (**-3**) for any Attacking Cavalry unit. The vulnerability to enemy Infantry and Artillery fire gives that enemy unit a **+1** and **+2** dice bonus respectively.

Operating the AI

The AI Chart
The AI Chart can be found on the page adjacent to each Battle Map and will look something like this:

AI: French	Roll **4 dice. Re-roll all duplicates under 6** (and all **6s if** Comm **not KIA**) once
Artillery (1)	**Set Up: Roll for Area; place on fourth hex down**
Attack nearest [Ar/Co/In/Cv] [TB2]	
3-5	Move horizontally downwards but only to put an enemy unit in Range *and* LoS [TB1]
6	Move straight down
Cavalry (2)	**Set Up: Roll for Area; place on fifth hex down**
Attack Co/In/Ar/Cv [TB2]	
3-4	Select nearest enemy Infantry unit. Move nearer to it [V] [TB1]: Attack Co/In/Ar/Cv [TB2]
	If no Infantry remain, Move nearer to the Objective [V] [TB1]: Attack Co/Ar/Cv [TB2]
5-6	If **T>2** select nearest enemy Infantry. Move nearer to it [H] [TB1]: Attack Co/In/Ar/Cv [TB2]
Infantry (3)	**Set Up: Roll for Area; place on second or third hex down**
If in Square & no enemy Cavalry within 3 hexes then De-Square: Attack nearest [Co/Ar/Cv/In] [TB2]	
If not in Square & enemy Cavalry are within 3 hexes then Square: Attack nearest [Co/Ar/Cv/In] [TB2]	
Attack nearest [Co/In/Cv/Ar] [TB2]	
1-2	If Objective is vacant Move nearer to it [H] [TB1]: Attack nearest [Co/Ar/Cv/In] [TB2]
3-4	If not already on a High Ground hex, select an *adjacent* vacant High Ground hex [nearest to Objective] [furthest down] [TB1]. Move onto it: Attack nearest [Co/Ar/Cv/In] [TB2]
5-6	Move straight down: Attack nearest [Co/Ar/Cv/In] [TB2]
Commander: General Henri François Delaborde	**Set Up: Roll for Area 2,3,4; place on top hex**
Attack In/Cv/Co/Ar [TB2]	
If Objective is vacant Move nearer to it [H] [TB1]: Attack In/Cv/Co/Ar [TB2]	
Select a vacant adjacent hex which is itself adjacent to *more* friendly units than the Commander is now [most friendly units] [furthest up] [TB1]. Move into it: Attack In/Cv/Co/Ar [TB2]	

[V] stands for Vertical and [H] stands for Horizontal. The effect of this is explained below, as are the abbreviations TB1 and TB2. Remember that the AI operates under the same basic rules as the Player and so, for example, will not Move when engaged in battle or when in Square formation. Note that each AI Chart has been created for its related Battle and there are significant differences between them. The main AI instructions are covered below under 'Operating the AI' and should allow the Player easily to interpret any other AI instructions included in the various Charts.

Setting Up the AI

Note that the Player will set up their units before the AI. However, the AI set up is dealt with here for convenience. General game set up is explained below under "Setting Up a Game".

The AI set up is straightforward. Units are set up in the order they appear in the AI Chart – Artillery, Cavalry, Infantry and then the Commander. Details of set up can be found in the AI Chart next to the name of each type of AI unit. For example, for Cavalry, the above AI Chart says **(2) Set Up: Roll for Area; place on fifth hex down**. The number in brackets tells the Player *how many* AI units of that type to place on the Map. In the example given, the Player would need to place 2 Cavalry units in total for the AI. The second part of the instruction then tells the Player where to set up those units. In the example given, for each of the 2 Cavalry units, the Player will roll a d6 (1 six sided die) to decide which of the AI's Areas the unit will start in (re-rolling 6s of course because there is no Area 6) and then place the Cavalry unit on the fifth hex down in that Area. Then the Player rolls for the next unit. If the resulting hex is occupied, then the Player re-rolls the die because 2 units can never occupy the same hex in this game. The Player continues until they have placed 2 Cavalry units on 2 different hexes.

For the Infantry in the above example Chart it says **(3) Set Up: Roll for Area; place on second or third hex down**. Again, the Player rolls for the Area for each Infantry unit and then rolls again to determine which of the two hexes the unit is placed on. If that hex is already occupied (by any unit) then the Player checks to see if the other hex is empty. If not, then the Player re-rolls for a different Area.

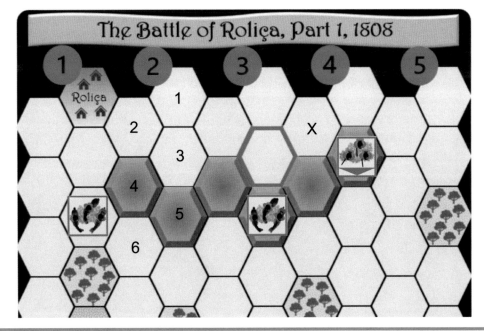

In the above example, the Player rolled a 1 and a 3 when setting up the AI's Cavalry, and so Cavalry units are placed on the fifth hex down in Areas 1 and 3. On set up, hexes in Areas are counted as shown in Area 2 above, alternating down the two columns that make up the Area in question. When setting up the Infantry, the Player rolled a 4 (Area 4) and then a 3 (number of Hexes down). If the Player rolls a 4 for the next Infantry unit, then it would automatically be placed on the second hex down in Area 4 (X) because this is the only option. If the Player rolls another 4 for the third Infantry unit, then they would need to re-roll as both permitted hexes in Area 4 are already occupied and more than one unit can never occupy the same hex.

Some instructions, as with the Commander in the example chart above, will restrict the Area in which the unit can set up. In the example, the Commander can only set up in **Area 2,3 or 4** and so the Player will re-roll until one of those numbers is displayed on the die.

The AI Turn – Selecting Areas

In much the same way as the player does on their Turn, the AI on its Turn will first need to select the Areas in which it will activate its units. This is done using the following procedure:

AI: French	Roll 4 dice. **Re-roll all duplicates under 6** (and all **6s** if Comm not KIA) once

A) **Roll 4 dice**. From the results, the AI will re-roll dice as follows:
- It will *always* re-roll any *duplicate* dice **under 6**.
- *If the AI Commander is still in play* it will re-roll **all 6s**.

All dice being re-rolled are rolled together and are only re-rolled once.

For example, if the AI initially rolls 3,3,5,6 then it will re-roll one of the 3s and, if the Commander is still alive, it will also re-roll the 6.

Once the final dice results are established, any remaining duplicates and 6s are discarded. In the above example, if the final dice results, after the re-roll, are 3,5,5,6, then one of the 5s and the 6 will be discarded.

B) Place each remaining die on its matching 'Area' number at the *top* of the page (the AI end). There will, of course, now only be one die (maximum) per Area. The AI will Activate, in this Turn, all of their units (if any) which are currently positioned anywhere in either of the two Columns of hexes making up each of the Areas into which a die has been placed. Note: it is possible that the AI could have dice on four different Areas if it gets lucky – something the Player can never do!

3 **1**

C) The AI will select the Areas (with dice allocated to them) in number order, from 1 to 5, and Activate each unit in that Area one by one, from bottom to top until all units in the Area have been Activated. Each unit will Move and/or Attack in accordance with the AI Chart shown on the page adjacent to each Battle Map (an example of which is produced earlier in this section of the rules).

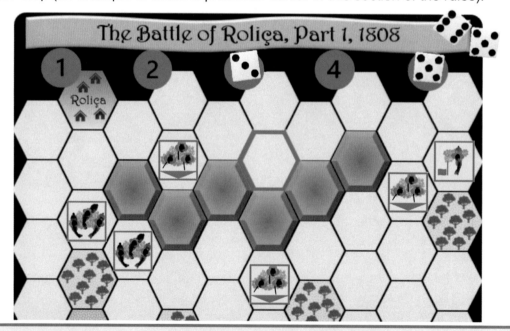

In the above example, the French AI has placed its dice and discarded the duplicate 5 and the 6. It will now Activate the Infantry unit in Area 3, followed by the two units in Area 5, Activating the Infantry unit before the Commander. It will then end its Turn. Note that it cannot Activate the Cavalry unit in Area 1 or the Infantry and Cavalry units in Area 2 this Turn.

The AI Turn – Activating the AI Units

The AI generally uses the same basic Move, Square and Attack rules as the Player. For example, any Move instruction is ignored if the AI unit is engaged in battle or in Square formation.

Tiebreaker rules

The AI Activation instructions often set out criteria to resolve any tie or choice in the AI decision-making process. A key part of that is making reference to the AI Tiebreaker Rules Chart which can be found on the page adjacent to each Battle Map. Note that this chart does change a little from Battle to Battle, but the following is a typical example.

The chart is split into two parts and each part applies in two different situations.

Move to which Hex? (referred to as **TB1** in the AI instructions)

This part of the chart applies where it has been established, under the AI instructions, that an AI unit has a choice of more than one hex to Move into (including when an AI unit is **retreating**).

Attack which Enemy? (referred to as **TB2** in the AI instructions)

This part of the chart applies where it has been established, under the AI instructions, that an AI unit has a choice of more than one enemy unit to Attack.

Only use these Charts when the AI instruction specifically refers to TB1 or TB2, or when an AI unit is **retreating** and has a choice of hexes to retreat into.

AI Tiebreaker Rules
TB1: Move to which Hex?
1. Within Range & LoS of enemy
2. Trees > Buildings hex
3. High Ground hex
4. Hex not in a River
5. Hex Furthest Up
6. In/nearest to Area 3
TB2: Attack which Enemy?
1. Unit nearest Objective
2. Unit Furthest Up
3. Unit not in Trees/Buildings
4. Strongest Unit

When using either part of the Chart, simply work down the relevant section until the criteria have solved the tiebreak. For example, if an AI unit has been instructed to Move nearer to a destination hex horizontally, and there are two hexes which are both horizontal to the AI unit *and* nearer to the destination hex than its current position, then the instruction is likely to then refer to TB1. So, (1) if one of the hexes put any enemy unit in Range and Line of Sight of the AI unit and the other did not, it will Move to where it could potentially Attack. If neither, or both, hexes provide a shot at an enemy unit, it will Move (2) to a Trees hex. If neither are Trees hexes it will Move to a Buildings hex. If neither are Trees/Buildings or both are Trees or both are Buildings, it will Move (3) onto a High Ground hex, then (4) *not* into a River, then (5) to the hex furthest up the Map and finally (6) the hex nearest to Area 3 (i.e., the most central hex). Of course, the 'tests' end as soon as the tiebreak is resolved.

If the tiebreak remains, which is unlikely, or if a particular instruction does not refer to TB1 or TB2, then decide the hex or unit randomly.

The AI Chart

Because the AI Chart for each Battle is specifically drafted for that Battle, the Player will see significant variation from one Battle to the next. However, the rules below and the examples that follow them should enable the Player to interpret each AI instruction correctly. Just do what it says – don't think!

When each unit is first Activated, find the section of the AI Chart that applies to that unit type and work through it from top to bottom, stopping once the AI has performed one of the instructions **in part or in full** (that is, it has actually Moved on the Map or changed formation and/or rolled some dice to try to Attack). The final section of many Charts require the Player to roll a die to determine the particular instruction to be performed by the AI unit. If *that* instruction cannot be performed, the AI unit's Activation ends there (do not re-roll for a different instruction at that point).

These **general rules** apply to the AI Activation instructions:

- Parts of an instruction which are after a colon (:) are *only* performed if the first part of the instruction was performed (in full or in part). This will generally be an Attack, after a Move or Square instruction.
- All information in square brackets [...] is for **tiebreak** purposes and should *only* be applied if there is a **choice** arising from the main instruction (because there is more than one unit or hex which satisfies the main instruction, for example). If there are two or more tiebreakers immediately after each other, consider them one by one until the tie is resolved.
- If the AI is instructed to Attack and it has a target but it turns out that it cannot roll any dice due to the Terrain or Situation modifiers, then it is deemed *not to have Attacked that unit* and will try to Attack the next valid target unit using the normal priority rules. For example, if an AI unit has an enemy Infantry unit and an enemy Cavalry unit in Range and Line of Sight but the modifiers mean it will roll no dice when Attacking its preferred unit, it will then try to Attack the *other* unit instead. If it cannot roll any dice to Attack *any* target unit, then:
  o If the Attack instruction is the solitary instruction that tends to come towards the beginning of each unit type's instructions, meaning it will not have performed any other instruction in full or in part, then it will continue to the next instruction.
  o If the Attack instruction comes after a *successful* Move or Square instruction then the unit will simply end its Activation in the usual way (because it has performed part of the instruction – the Move or Square).
- Up, Down, Left and Right are always interpreted from the Players viewpoint of the Map.
- Cavalry will always try to Move up to 2 hexes (one at a time) unless otherwise stated.

Here is an example of an Infantry section of the AI Chart:

Infantry (3)	Set Up: Roll for Area; place on third or, if occupied, second hex down
If in Square & no enemy Cavalry within 3 hexes then De-Square: Attack nearest [Co/Ar/Cv/In] [TB2]	
If not in Square & enemy Cavalry are within 3 hexes then Square: Attack nearest [Co/Ar/Cv/In] [TB2]	
Attack nearest [Co/In/Cv/Ar] [TB2]	
1-2	If Objective is vacant Move nearer to it [H] [TB1]: Attack nearest [Co/Ar/Cv/In] [TB2]
3-4	If not already on a High Ground hex, select an *adjacent* vacant High Ground hex [nearest to Objective] [furthest down] [TB1]. Move onto it: Attack nearest [Co/Ar/Cv/In] [TB2]
5-6	Move straight down: Attack nearest [Co/Ar/Cv/In] [TB2]

When an Infantry unit Activates using this example Chart, the Player would **first** determine whether that unit is in Square formation and if so, consider whether there are any enemy (Player) Cavalry within three hexes of that Infantry unit. If not, then the unit would come out of Square formation. It would then try to Attack the nearest enemy unit (in Range and Line of Sight). Only if there is more than one enemy unit *equidistant* from it would it consider the tiebreak information in square brackets, meaning it would choose the enemy Commander (Co) first, then an Artillery unit (Ar), then a Cavalry unit (Cv) and finally an Infantry unit (In). Remember, it will *only* consider that tiebreak information if the main instruction does not produce a clear result. If there is only one unit that is nearest to the AI Infantry, then it will Attack that unit, regardless of what it is. It would *not* Attack an enemy Commander three hexes away if there is an Infantry unit two hexes away, even though both are in Range and Line of Sight – the Infantry would be the *nearest* unit (unless, of course, modifiers meant no dice would be rolled when Attacking the Infantry – see the General AI Rules above). If there are two units of the *same type* equidistant from the Infantry unit, then reference would be made to the Tiebreaker chart – section TB2 as stated in square brackets. Also, remember that it will only try to Attack in this first instruction if it came out of square formation – **the part after a colon is only ever attempted if the first part of the instruction was performed**. Whether the Attack is performed or not, the unit's Activation would end if it performed the first part of the instruction.

If the Infantry unit is not in Square formation, or it is in Square formation and there is an enemy Cavalry unit within three hexes, then the first instruction would fail. It would also fail if the Infantry unit was engaged in battle as in that case it cannot change formation. It would therefore go on to consider the second instruction.

The **second** instruction applies if the AI Infantry unit is *not* in Square formation and there *is* an enemy Cavalry unit within three hexes. If so, it will go into Square formation and then try to Attack in the same way as explained above.

If neither of the first two instructions can be performed, then the **third** instruction requires the Infantry unit to Attack the nearest enemy, again in the same way as explained above. Note that the tiebreaker sequence is a little different this time, in terms of the priority of units to Attack if there is a tie, but again it only comes into effect if there are two or more enemy units which are all *nearest* to *and* equidistant from the AI Infantry unit.

If no Attack is possible, then the **fourth** and final section of the Chart requires a die to be rolled, with the result determining what the AI Infantry unit will try to do. If the resulting instruction cannot be performed, the die is not re-rolled and the unit's Activation comes to an end. Similarly, if a number is rolled which is not included in the Chart (impossible in this particular example) then the unit will do nothing and its Activation will end.

On the roll of a 1 or 2, the AI Infantry unit in this example will Move one hex nearer to the Objective, as long as the Objective is currently unoccupied by any unit. Whenever a unit is required to Move **nearer to** something in this game, it will only Move if by doing so it **reduces** the distance in hexes between itself and the 'target' it is Moving nearer to. This means the **most direct distance** (as the crow flies, so to speak) and **not** the shortest clear path around other units. The tiebreak in square brackets [H] requires that if there are two or more possible target hexes which are all nearer to the Objective then the unit will Move **horizontally** which means that it will Move to one of the two columns adjacent to it rather than up or down its existing column (which would be a **vertical** [V] Move). Of course, it will Move vertically if that is the only way to get nearer to the Objective. If, despite this tiebreak, the Infantry unit still has a choice of two or more hexes to Move to, then the AI Tiebreaker Rules Chart (TB1) should be referred to. If it *can* Move nearer to the Objective, then it will try to perform the second part of the instruction, which requires it to Attack the nearest unit. If there are two or more units which are equidistant from the AI Infantry unit, then it will use the tiebreak information in square brackets to decide which unit type to Attack. If there is more than one of the same type equidistant away, then the TB2 section of the AI Tiebreaker Rules Chart should be used.

On a roll of 3 or 4, the AI Infantry unit will Move one hex onto an *adjacent* High Ground hex but only if it is not already on a High Ground hex. The first step is to identify the relevant hex to Move to. If it has a choice of adjacent vacant High Ground hexes then in this example it will select the hex which is nearest to the Objective and if this does not resolve the tiebreak it will select the hex furthest down the Battle Map (from the Player's perspective). If there is still a tie, it will use the TB1 section of the AI Tiebreaker Rules Chart. Only then will it Move onto the identified hex. Always read the instruction carefully. Note that here the unit will *only* Move if it can Move *onto* an *adjacent* High Ground hex. This instruction does not allow the unit generally to Move *nearer* to a High Ground hex which is more than one hex away. If it cannot Move *onto* a High Ground hex for any reason or is already on a High Ground hex, it will not Move under this instruction and its Activation ends. If it does Move, then it will try to Attack the nearest unit as previously explained.

On a roll of 5 or 6, the AI Infantry unit will simply Move one hex **straight down** the Battle Map. This means it will *only* Move *straight down the column it is currently occupying*. If its path is blocked, it will not Move. If it does Move, it will then Attack the nearest unit as previously explained.

Moving on to an example of the **Cavalry** section of an AI Chart:

Cavalry (2)	Set Up: Roll for Area; place on fifth hex down
Attack Co/In/Ar/Cv [TB2]	
3-4	Select nearest enemy Infantry [furthest up]. Move nearer to it [V] [TB1]: Attack Co/In/Ar/Cv [TB2] If no Infantry remain, Move nearer to the Objective [V] [TB1]: Attack Co/Ar/Cv [TB2]
5-6	If **T>2** select nearest enemy. Move nearer to it [H] [TB1]: Attack Co/In/Ar/Cv [TB2]

When a Cavalry unit Activates using this example Chart, the Player would **first** determine whether the Cavalry unit can Attack any enemy unit. As the Cavalry unit has a Range of one hex, it does not Attack the *nearest* unit, as all possible targets can only be one hex away. The instruction therefore jumps straight into a priority order. Note that this is not in square brackets as it is not a tiebreaker as such but part of the key instruction. Here, it will always Attack the enemy Commander if possible, and if not, it will Attack an enemy Infantry unit, then an Artillery unit and finally an enemy Cavalry unit. Remember, this order varies from instruction to instruction so always check it carefully. If there is more than one unit of the same type adjacent to the Cavalry unit then it will use the TB2 AI Tiebreaker Rules Chart to determine the target. If it can Attack, its Activation will of course end here.

If no Attack is possible, then the **second** and final section of the Chart requires a die to be rolled, with the result determining what the AI Cavalry unit will try to do. As always, if the resulting instruction cannot be performed, the die is not re-rolled and the unit's Activation comes to an end. And again, if a number is rolled which is not included in the Chart (in this example, a 1 or 2) then the unit will do nothing and its Activation will end.

On a roll of 3 or 4, the AI Cavalry unit will Move up to two hexes (its Movement value) nearer to the nearest enemy Infantry unit. The first step, as stated in the instruction, is to identify the nearest enemy Infantry unit. The tiebreaker is to take the Infantry unit which is furthest up the Battle Map. If more than one satisfies this test, then decide it randomly (the TB1 and TB2 AI Tiebreaker Rules Charts do not cover this situation). Once that 'target' enemy Infantry unit is selected, this will not change for any reason whilst the AI Cavalry perform this instruction, even if the Cavalry cannot actually Move any nearer to it. Perform each of the Cavalry unit's 2 Moves individually. *For each Move in turn*, identify the possible adjacent destination hexes which the Cavalry unit can validly Move to which are *nearer* to the target Infantry unit. If there is none, then its Activation ends. Remember, the Cavalry cannot perform its second Move if it Moves adjacent to *any* Player unit on its first Move. Similarly, it will not perform its second Move if its route is blocked by other units. Note that in this sample AI Chart, on a 3-4 Cavalry prefer *vertical* [V] Moves when they have a choice of hexes to Move to, so that they will Move straight down (or possibly up) their existing column in preference to Moving to a new column, but remember they must always Move *nearer* to the target enemy unit – this applies to *both* of their Moves. If a vertical Move does not get them nearer, then the unit will try a horizontal Move. If a choice of hexes arises despite this tiebreaker, then use the TB1 chart as stated. Once they have Moved they will try to Attack an adjacent unit in the preferred order stated in the Chart, using TB2 as necessary if two or more of the same unit type are in Range (this may not be the original 'target' infantry). If they Move (whether they then Attack or not) the unit's Activation will end here. If no enemy Infantry remain, the instruction requires the Cavalry to Move nearer to the Objective (preferring vertical Moves if there is a choice) and then Attack if possible (again, charts TB1 and TB2 apply as needed).

On a roll of 5-6 the instruction is the same, but the Cavalry unit will select the nearest *unit* (not just Infantry). Decide randomly if there is more than one equidistant from the Cavalry unit. When it Moves, it will prefer *horizontal* [H] Moves – to an adjacent column, but again it *must* take the Cavalry *nearer* to the enemy unit. As ever, if a horizontal Move would not do this (because the two units are in the same column) then it will Move vertically if it can, and if that takes it nearer to the enemy unit. Again, the Cavalry unit will try to Attack if it does Move, as previously explained. Note also that this instruction is only carried out if the game is currently on a **Turn (T)** which is *greater than* 2, that is, <u>on</u> **Turn 3 or higher**. On Turns 1 and 2 the instruction is simply ignored and the Cavalry unit's Activation ends.

Looking at an example of the Artillery section of an AI Chart:

Artillery (1)	Set Up: Roll for Area; place on fourth hex down
Attack nearest [Ar/Co/In/Cv] [TB2]	
3-5	Move horizontally downwards but only to put an enemy unit in Range *and* LoS [TB1]
6	Move straight down

As was the case with Cavalry units, and will often be the case with other types of unit, in this example the Artillery unit will, when activated, **first** try to Attack the *nearest* enemy unit. Again, the priority is to attack the *nearest* unit and only if there is more than one enemy unit equidistant away from the Artillery unit (in Range and Line of Sight of course) will it need to refer to the tiebreak sequence shown in square brackets and then to TB2. Remember that Artillery have Line of Sight (LoS) along straight lines of hexes only in the six directions from its hex. If it can Attack, its Activation will of course end here.

If no Attack is possible, then the **second** (and final) section of the Chart requires a die to be rolled, with the result determining what the AI Artillery unit will try to do. As always, if the resulting instruction cannot be performed, the die is not re-rolled and the unit's Activation comes to an end. And again, if a number is rolled which is not included in the Chart (in this example, a 1 or 2) then the unit will do nothing and its Activation will end.

On a roll of 3,4 or 5, in this example the Artillery unit will Move one hex *horizontally downwards* to the left or right. Note that because the instruction specifically states that it Moves horizontally *and* downwards, then it will only Move in that way. It cannot, under this instruction, Move straight down its column (vertically) or Move *up* the Battle Map in any way. It would usually have two possible hexes to Move to (as shown) but may only have one if it is currently on the very edge of the Battle Map. It will only Move if it can get an enemy unit in Range *and* Line of Sight from the hex it Moves to. This instruction does not allow the unit to try to Move nearer to a Player unit (the instruction does not refer to Moving *nearer* to anything). If both hexes would result in an enemy unit being in Range and Line of Sight then the hex to Move to would be decided using the TB1: 'Move to which Hex?' section of the separate AI Tiebreaker Rules chart (see earlier).

In this example, if the French Artillery unit rolls a 3,4 or 5 it can only Move to either of the two indicated hexes, being those hexes which are *both* horizontal *and* downward of the unit's current hex.

In fact it will Move to the Higher Ground hex as this puts the British Infantry unit within its Range *and* Line of Sight.

If this was not possible (because the British unit was not there or would be out of Line of Sight, or the Higher Ground hex was already occupied by another unit) then the Artillery unit would not Move at all under this instruction.

In some Battles the AI instructions may require the Artillery to Move horizontally downwards to the **right**, or to Move horizontally downwards to the **left**. Again, it would then only Move in that exact direction. As stated earlier, the 'right' or 'left' refers to the Player's point of view (so towards the right or to the left of the Map as the Player looks at it), not from the point of view of the AI unit itself.

On a roll of 6, the Artillery unit will simply Move one hex straight down the Battle Map (in the same column it is in). If that one hex is already occupied by any other unit, the Artillery will not Move.

Looking at an example of the Commander section of an AI Chart:

Commander: Sir Arthur Wellesley	Set Up: Roll for Areas 2,3,4; place on top hex
Attack In/Cv/Co/Ar [TB2]	
If **T > 7** then Move nearer to the Objective [V] [TB1]: Attack In/Cv/Co/Ar [TB2]	
Select a vacant adjacent hex which is itself adjacent to *more* friendly units than the Commander is now [most friendly units] [furthest up] [TB1]. Move into it: Attack In/Cv/Co/Ar [TB2]	
Select the nearest *friendly* unit [In/Ar/Cv] [furthest up]. Move nearer to it [H] [TB1]: Attack In/Cv/Co/Ar [TB2]	

As with other unit types, the Commander will usually try to Attack **first**. Commanders are always treated as a (one strength) Cavalry unit and so can only Attack adjacent units. The instruction contains the order in which he will prefer to Attack given a choice. TB2 is to be used if needed.

In the above example, if the Commander cannot Attack, then the **second** instruction only applies if the **Turn (T)** counter is *greater than* 7 (in other words, it is Turn 8, 9 or 10). In that case, the Commander will try to Move nearer to the Objective and if he has a choice of hexes then he will prefer to Move vertically [V] rather than horizontally, but as previously explained, he will Move horizontally if that is the only way to get nearer to the Objective. As with Cavalry units, perform each of the two Moves individually and the Commander will only Move each time if he can get nearer to the Objective **on that Move**. If he Moves at all then he will try to Attack, with the preference order of target unit again set out in the instruction itself.

If the Turn counter is 7 or below, or if the Commander cannot move *nearer* to the Objective, then the **third** instruction requires the Commander to try to Move (but only to an *adjacent* hex) in order to then get adjacent to *more* friendly units than he is currently adjacent to. As usual, follow the instructions carefully – first, find all *vacant hexes adjacent* to the Commander's current position which are themselves adjacent to more friendly units than the Commander is currently adjacent to. If there is more than one such hex, then he will choose the one which is adjacent to the *most* friendly units and then the hex which is furthest up the Battle Map. If needed, reference should then be made to the TB1 section of the AI Tiebreaker Rules Chart. Once the destination hex is established, then he will Move into that hex. If no such hexes exist, then the instruction fails – go on to the next instruction. If he does Move then he will try to Attack as usual, then his Activation will end.

If the Commander does not Move under the third instruction, then the **fourth** instruction requires him to Move nearer to the nearest friendly unit. Of course, if he is already adjacent to a friendly unit, then he will not Move at this stage because he cannot get any nearer than that. As ever, follow the instruction carefully. First, select the nearest friendly unit. If there is a choice of units, then the instruction provides the preferred order of units that should be selected, and if a tiebreak remains then the unit furthest up the Battle Map will be selected. The Commander will then try to Move *nearer* to that unit and if there is a choice of hexes to Move to at this stage, he would prefer to Move horizontally [H]. If he cannot Move nearer to that unit, his Activation will end because this is the final instruction for the Commander (remember, do *not* select a different 'target' unit). If he does Move, again he will try to attack. As ever, use Charts TB1 and TB2 when they are referred to, to resolve remaining tie breaks.

Examples of AI Orders

Example 1 – AI Movement

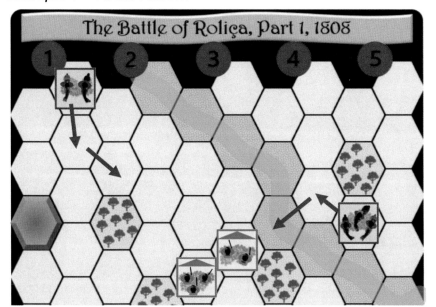

AI Tiebreaker Rules	
TB1: Move to which Hex?	
1. Within Range & LoS of enemy	
2. Trees > Buildings hex	
3. High Ground hex	
4. Hex not in a River	
5. Hex Furthest Down	
6. In/nearest to Area 3	
TB2: Attack which Enemy?	
1. Unit Furthest Up	
2. Unit not in Trees	
3. Strongest Unit	
4. Unit in/nearest to Area 3	

Cavalry (2)	Set Up: Roll for Area; place on fifth hex down
Attack Co/In/Ar/Cv [TB2]	
3-4	Select nearest enemy Infantry [furthest up]. Move nearer to it [V][TB1]: Attack Co/In/Ar/Cv [TB2] If no Infantry remain, Move nearer to the Objective [V] [TB1]: Attack Co/Ar/Cv [TB2]

Much of the time, the concept of 'horizontal' [H] and 'vertical' [V] Movement, and the preferences for each that AI units have, will resolve the issue of which hex a unit should Move to. The AI's two strength Cavalry unit above cannot Attack, and so it rolls a die. Assuming it rolls a 4, it must try to Move up to 2 hexes (its Movement value) nearer to the nearest enemy Infantry unit. As both Infantry units are five hexes away, it uses the tiebreak in the instruction itself (in square brackets) and selects the Infantry unit furthest up the Map (the two strength Infantry unit). If both units were on the exact same row of hexes, then the Player would decide the unit randomly (the separate AI Tiebreaker Rules Charts TB1 and TB2 do not apply in such situations).

When it Moves, it will Move vertically downwards on its first Move because that takes it *nearer* to the 'target' unit and it prefers vertical [V] Moves (as set out in the instruction itself). On its second Move it will Move horizontally because although it would prefer to Move vertically, this will no longer take it *nearer* to the two strength French Infantry unit it is heading towards.

Assuming the three strength Cavalry also rolls a 4, then it will Move nearer to the nearest (two strength) Infantry unit. Clearly, on this occasion, it needs to Move horizontally, as a vertical Move (up or down its own column) will not take it *nearer* to the Infantry. It has a choice of 2 hexes – the River hex or the Clear hex above it. Using the separate Tiebreaker Rules Chart it will Move into the Clear hex as those Rules (at point 4) tell it to avoid the River hex (points 1-3 do not solve the tiebreak). On its second Move, it will Move adjacent to the Infantry unit, and must Move into the River hex because this is the only way it can Move *nearer* to the target infantry unit (no tiebreaker is needed). It would then, of course, Attack that Infantry unit under the second part of the instruction (suffering a 1 die penalty to its Attack for being in a River hex).

Example 2 – AI Movement

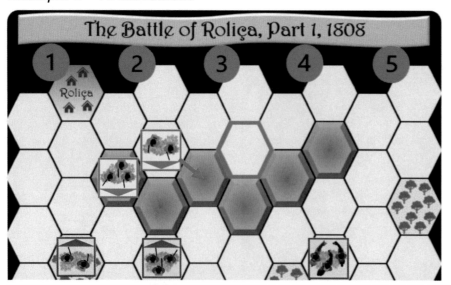

The Battle of Roliça, Part 1, 1808

AI Tiebreaker Rules
TB1: Move to which Hex?
1. Within Range & LoS of enemy
2. Trees > Buildings hex
3. High Ground hex
4. Hex not in a River
5. Hex Furthest Up
6. In/nearest to Area 3
TB2: Attack which Enemy?
1. Unit nearest Objective
2. Unit Furthest Up
3. Unit not in Trees/Buildings
4. Strongest Unit

Infantry	(5) Set Up: Place on second hex down of Areas 2,3,4 and third hex down of Areas 2,3
	If in Square & no enemy Cavalry within 3 hexes then De-Square: Attack nearest [Co/Ar/Cv/In] [TB2]
	If not in Square & enemy Cavalry are within 3 hexes then Square: Attack nearest [Co/Ar/Cv/In] [TB2]
	Attack nearest [Co/In/Cv/Ar] [TB2]
1-2	If Objective is vacant Move nearer to it [H] [TB1]: Attack nearest [Co/Ar/Cv/In] [TB2]
3-4	If not already on a High Ground hex, select an *adjacent* vacant High Ground hex [nearest to Objective] [furthest down] [TB1]. Move onto it: Attack nearest [Co/Ar/Cv/In] [TB2]

If the AI French Infantry units were in square formation, they would both come out of Square formation under the first instruction because the only enemy Cavalry unit is more than 3 hexes away. If so, they would then try to Attack one of the enemy Infantry units under the second part of the instruction (the Cavalry is clearly out of Range/Line of Sight). The three strength Infantry unit can Attack either of the enemy British Infantry units. Using the TB2 section of the AI Tiebreaker Rules Chart, the 'Attack which Enemy?' section tells us that they will Attack the unit nearest the Objective (blue hex) – the three strength British unit. The AI's two strength Infantry does not have Line of Sight to either British Infantry unit, which is blocked by High Ground hexes. In both cases, the unit would then end its Activation as at least part of the Order would have been performed (coming out of Square formation).

Assuming neither is in Square, so the first instruction does not apply, they will *not* go into Square formation under the second instruction because the Player's Cavalry unit is more than 3 hexes away.

In that case, the three strength Infantry unit would Attack under the third instruction, targeting the Player's Infantry unit nearest to the Objective for the reasons set out above. The two strength Infantry unit cannot Attack and so will need to go on to the final section and roll a die.

Assuming it rolls a 1 or 2, it will Move 1 hex nearer the Objective, because it is vacant. Both possible hexes nearer to the Objective involve horizontal Moves, so that particular tiebreaker in the instruction itself does not help. Tiebreaker Chart TB1 tells us (at step 1) that the unit will Move to be in Range and Line of Sight of an enemy unit. It would then Attack the three strength British Infantry unit which it can now see. In fact, if the unit rolled a 3 or 4 it would end up on the same hex because it would Move onto an adjacent vacant Higher Ground hex and prefer the hex nearest to the Objective (as stated in the 3-4 instruction itself). Again, it will then Attack the same British unit, being the nearest unit.

Example 3 – AI Movement

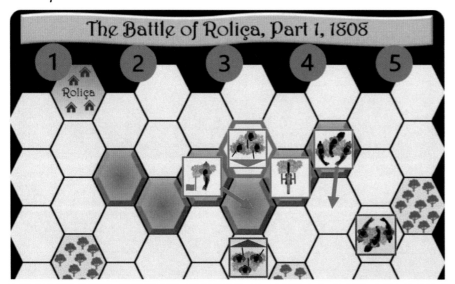

AI Tiebreaker Rules					
TB1: Move to which Hex?					
1. Within Range & LoS of enemy					
2. Trees > Buildings hex					
3. High Ground hex					
4. Hex not in a River					
5. Hex Furthest Up					
6. In/nearest to Area 3					
TB2: Attack which Enemy?					
1. Unit nearest Objective					
2. Unit Furthest Up					
3. Unit not in Trees/Buildings					
4. Strongest Unit					

Commander: General Henri François Delaborde	**Set Up: Roll for Areas 2,3,4; place on top hex**
Attack In/Cv/Co/Ar [TB2]	
If Objective is vacant Move nearer to it [H] [TB1]: Attack In/Cv/Co/Ar [TB2]	
Select a vacant adjacent hex which is itself adjacent to *more* friendly units than the Commander is now [most friendly units] [furthest up] [TB1]. Move into it: Attack In/Cv/Co/Ar [TB2]	

Cavalry (2) Set Up:	**Roll for Areas 1,2,4,5; place on sixth hex down**
Attack Co/In/Ar/Cv [TB2]	
3-4	Select nearest enemy Infantry [furthest up]. Move nearer to it [V][TB1]: Attack Co/In/Ar/Cv [TB2] If no enemy Infantry remain, Move nearer to the Objective [V] [TB1]: Attack Co/Ar/Cv [TB2]

The AI French Commander cannot Attack under the first instruction as there is no adjacent unit. The Objective is not vacant and so the second instruction does not apply either. The third instruction tries to direct the Commander to an adjacent hex which puts him adjacent to *more* friendly units than is currently the case. He is currently adjacent to one unit. There is only one vacant adjacent hex which satisfies the basic test in this instruction The selected hex will therefore be the (High Ground) hex that puts him adjacent to the French Infantry and Artillery as shown by the blue arrow above. Once the hex is selected he will Move into it (he will be able to do this because the selected hex will always be adjacent and vacant). After he Moves, he will then Attack the British Infantry unit in the usual way.

The AI French Cavalry unit cannot Attack and so it will roll a die. Assuming it rolls a 3, then it will try to Move nearer to the nearest enemy Infantry unit – there is only one Infantry unit and so the tiebreaker in the instruction itself (furthest up) is not required. When it Moves, it will prefer to Move vertically if possible, which it can do, as this takes it *nearer* to the 'target' Infantry unit. However, after its first Move it will then be engaged in battle with the Player's Cavalry unit and so it cannot make its second Move (it cannot Move at all – except to retreat when Attacked – until those units are no longer engaged). The second part of the instruction requires it to Attack, and so it will then Attack the Player's Cavalry unit to which it is now adjacent of course.

Example 4 – AI Attacks

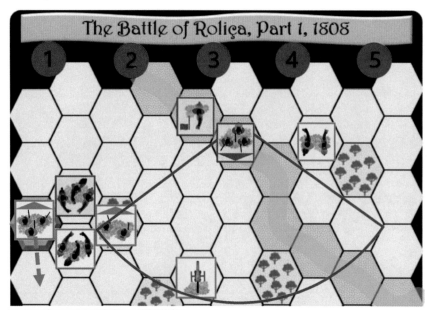

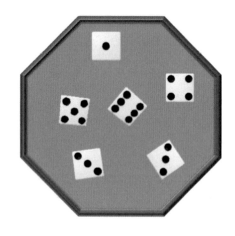

Situation or Terrain ((Units, High Ground & Buildings block LoS)	Dice	AI Tiebreaker Rules
Infantry attacking **at _Range 1_ after Moving**	+1	**TB1: Move to which Hex?**
Infantry attacking **at _Range 2-3_ after Moving**	-1	1. Within Range & LoS of enemy
Infantry attacking **at _Range 2-3_ whilst in Square formation**	-1	2. Trees > Buildings hex
Infantry attacking Infantry **who are in Square formation**	+1	3. High Ground hex
Cavalry attacking Infantry **who are in Square formation**	-3	4. Hex not in a River
Artillery attacking **at Range 1-3**	+2	5. Hex Furthest Down
Artillery attacking Infantry **who are in Square formation**	+2	6. In/nearest to Area 3
Any unit attacking **which is adjacent to its** Commander	+1	**TB2: Attack which Enemy?**
Any unit attacking **from Higher Ground than its Target**	+1	1. Unit Furthest Up
Any unit attacking **a unit in Trees or Buildings**	-1	2. Unit not in Trees
Any unit attacking **through intervening Trees**	-1	3. Strongest Unit
Any unit attacking **from a River hex**	-1	4. Unit in/nearest to Area 3

Cavalry (2)	Set Up: Roll for Area; place on fifth hex down
Attack Co/In/Ar/Cv [TB2]	
Infantry (6)	Set Up: Roll for Area; place on third or, if occupied, second hex down
Attack nearest [Co/In/Cv/Ar] [TB2]	

Unit	M	R	Units cannot Move if Square/engaged in battle	v Inf	v Cav	v Art
Infantry	1	3	Move or Square/De-Square, then Attack	4 - 3 - 2	3 - 2 - 2	3 - 2 - 2
Cavalry	2	1	Move, then Attack	6 - 5 - 4	4 - 3 - 2	4 - 3 - 2
Artillery	1	6	Move or Attack	3 - 2	2 - 1	2 - 1

The AI British Cavalry unit has a choice of 3 adjacent units to Attack. The instruction itself dictates that it will Attack Infantry before Cavalry. Of the 2 Infantry units, it will prefer the unit *not* in Trees under the TB2 section of the AI Tiebreaker Rules Chart (step 2). It will roll 6 dice to Attack (the High Ground hex has no effect on a defending unit). Assuming it rolls **1,3,3,4,5,6** then the Infantry unit will be reduced to one strength (**5,6**) and will retreat one hex straight down the Battle Map (**4**).

The AI British Infantry unit can Attack the two strength Player Infantry unit or the Player Artillery unit. It cannot Attack the Cavalry because it is outside its arc of fire (shown in red). Both targets are 3 hexes away, so the tiebreaker in the instruction itself means it will Attack the Infantry unit in preference to the Artillery. It will roll 3 dice in total – the basic Attack for a three strength Infantry unit against Infantry is 4 dice, plus 1 die because the Attacker is adjacent to their Commander, less 1 because the target unit is in a Trees hex and less 1 because the Attacker is in a River hex.

Setting Up a Game

These are the steps to follow to set up a new game:

1. Select a Battle to play.
2. Set up the Player's units first. The number of each unit available for the Battle is set out in the Player Chart:

Player: British & Portuguese		Place each Unit below the red dashed line	
Infantry: 5	Cavalry: 2	Artillery: 1	Commander: Sir Arthur Wellesley
Roll 3 dice. **Re-roll any dice once** (all together). **If Commander not KIA**, then 6s are Wild			

   Follow the Set Up instructions, which usually (but not always) means setting up the Player's units towards the bottom of the Battle Map, below a dashed line shown on the Map. It is perfectly acceptable to peruse the AI Set Up instructions for clues as to their formation.
3. Set up the AI in accordance with the instructions given above in the 'Setting Up the AI' part of the section on 'Operating the AI'. As a reminder, the number of each unit and the set up instructions are found in the AI Chart alongside the name of each type of unit.
4. Place a counter on, or in some other way mark, the Turn Tracker at Turn 1.

Adjusting the Difficulty

The Battles do vary in difficulty but the Player is left to discover this for themselves! If you find any particular Battle too easy or too difficult, feel free to adjust the starting units of the armies. One more or fewer unit can make a significant difference!

Order of Play Summary

Most of this can be found on the page adjacent to each Battle Map.

1. Place each of your own units in the starting area below the dashed line, or as otherwise explained on the page adjacent to each Battle Map.
2. Place the AI units in accordance with the set up instructions for the Battle.
3. Place a counter on, or mark, the next Turn Tracker section.
4. Activate Player units:
   Roll **3** dice. Re-roll any number of those dice once (and all together). Discard any duplicates under 6. Discard all 6s if your Commander is killed in action. If not, then 6s are Wild and can be changed to any face not already displayed on another die. Place each remaining die on the matching Area number. Then, taking each Area in turn in any order, Activate each unit within each Area (again in any order) and Move/Square/Attack as permitted.
5. Activate enemy units:
   Roll **4** dice. Re-roll all duplicates under 6, and also all 6s if the AI Commander is not killed in action. Discard any remaining duplicates and 6s and then allocate the remaining dice to their matching Areas. Taking each Area in order 1-5, Activate every AI unit in the Area from bottom to top. Perform the instructions as set out in the relevant AI chart for the Battle.
6. If the Turn Tracker is not full, go back to Step 3.

At all times keep checking whether the Objective has been achieved. Remember, total elimination of the enemy army always results in immediate victory, regardless of the actual Objective stated.

THE BATTLES...

1. The Battle of Roliça - Part 1, 17 August 1808 (British/Portuguese)

In the first Battle fought by the British in the Peninsular war, the British and Portuguese army secured victory with the French retiring in good order. In reality, the French were vastly outnumbered, but the armies have been levelled up here to provide more of a challenge. Sir Arthur Wellesley later became the Duke of Wellington. *This Map (only) has a reminder in Area 2 of how to count hexes on AI set up.*

Objective: *Occupy the blue outlined objective hex with any unit at any time.*

Player: British & Portuguese	Place each Unit below the red dashed line		
Infantry: 5	Cavalry: 2	Artillery: 1	Commander: Sir Arthur Wellesley
Roll **3** dice. **Re-roll any dice once** (all together). **If** Commander **not KIA**, then 6s are Wild			

AI: French	Roll **4** dice. **Re-roll all duplicates under 6** (and all **6s** if Comm not KIA) once
Artillery (1)	**Set Up: Roll for Area; place on fourth hex down**
Attack nearest [Ar/Co/In/Cv] [TB2]	
3-5	Move horizontally downwards, but only to put an enemy unit in Range *and* LoS [TB1]
6	Move straight down
Cavalry (2)	**Set Up: Roll for Area; place on fifth hex down**
Attack Co/In/Ar/Cv [TB2]	
3-4	Select nearest enemy Infantry [furthest up]. Move nearer to it [V][TB1]: Attack Co/In/Ar/Cv [TB2] If no enemy Infantry remain, Move nearer to the Objective [V][TB1]: Attack Co/Ar/Cv [TB2]
5-6	If **T>2** select nearest [furthest up] enemy. Move nearer to it [H][TB1]: Attack Co/In/Ar/Cv [TB2]
Infantry (5) Set Up: Place on second hex down of Areas 2,3,4 and third hex down of Areas 2,3	
If in Square & no enemy Cavalry within 3 hexes then De-Square: Attack nearest [Co/Ar/Cv/In] [TB2]	
If not in Square & enemy Cavalry are within 3 hexes then Square: Attack nearest [Co/Ar/Cv/In] [TB2]	
Attack nearest [Co/In/Cv/Ar] [TB2]	
1-2	If Objective is vacant Move nearer to it [H] [TB1]: Attack nearest [Co/Ar/Cv/In] [TB2]
3-4	If not already on a High Ground hex, select an *adjacent* vacant High Ground hex [nearest to Objective] [furthest down] [TB1]. Move onto it: Attack nearest [Co/Ar/Cv/In] [TB2]
5-6	Move straight down: Attack nearest [Co/Ar/Cv/In] [TB2]
Commander: General Henri François Delaborde **Set Up: Roll for Area 2,3,4; place on top hex**	
Attack In/Cv/Co/Ar [TB2]	
If Objective is vacant Move nearer to it [adjacent to most friendly units] [TB1]: Attack In/Cv/Co/Ar [TB2]	
Select a vacant adjacent hex which is itself adjacent to *more* friendly units than the Commander is now [most friendly units] [furthest up] [TB1]. Move into it: Attack In/Cv/Co/Ar [TB2]	

Unit	M	R	Units cannot Move if Square/engaged in battle	v Inf	v Cav	v Art
Infantry	1	3	Move or Square/De-Square, then Attack	4 - 3 - 2	3 - 2 - 2	3 - 2 - 2
Cavalry	2	1	Move, then Attack	6 - 5 - 4	4 - 3 - 2	4 - 3 - 2
Artillery	1	6	Move or Attack	3 - 2	2 - 1	2 - 1

Situation or Terrain (Units, High Ground & Buildings block LoS)	Dice	AI Tiebreaker Rules
Infantry attacking **at Range 1 after Moving**	+1	**TB1: Move to which Hex?**
Infantry attacking **at Range 2-3 after Moving**	-1	1. Within Range & LoS of enemy
Infantry attacking **at Range 2-3 whilst in Square formation**	-1	2. Trees > Buildings hex
Infantry attacking Infantry **who are in Square formation**	+1	3. High Ground hex
Cavalry attacking Infantry **who are in Square formation**	-3	4. Hex not in a River
Artillery attacking **at Range 1-3**	+2	5. Hex Furthest Up
Artillery attacking Infantry **who are in Square formation**	+2	6. In/nearest to Area 3
Any unit attacking which is adjacent to its Commander	+1	**TB2: Attack which Enemy?**
Any unit attacking from Higher Ground than its Target	+1	1. Unit nearest Objective
Any unit attacking a unit in Trees or Buildings	-1	2. Unit Furthest Up
Any unit attacking through intervening Trees	-1	3. Unit not in Trees/Buildings
Any unit attacking from a River hex	-1	4. Strongest Unit

1. The Battle of Roliça, Part 1, 1808

Turn [1][2][3][4][5][6][7][8][9][10]

2. The Battle of Roliça - Part 1, 17 August 1808 (French)

The British and Portuguese army secured victory with the French retiring in good order. The French were actually vastly outnumbered, as in this scenario, so see how you get on here as the 'defender'.

Objective: *Prevent the British & Portuguese from occupying the shaded Higher Ground hex (the "Objective") at any time.*

Player: French	Place each Unit below the blue dashed line		
Infantry: 3	Cavalry: 2	Artillery: 1	Commander: General Henri François Delaborde
Roll 3 dice. Re-roll any dice once (all together). If Commander not KIA, then 6s are Wild			

AI: British/Portuguese	Roll 4 dice. Re-roll all duplicates under 6 (and all 6s if Comm not KIA) once
Artillery (1)	**Set Up: Roll for Area; place on second hex down**
Attack nearest [Ar/Co/In/Cv] [TB2]	
1-3	Move horizontally downwards but only to put an enemy unit in Range *and* LoS [TB1]
4-6	Move straight down
Cavalry (4)	**Set Up: Place on fifth and sixth hexes down of Area 1 and fourth and fifth hexes down of Area 5**
Attack Co/In/Ar/Cv [TB2]	
If **T > 6** then Move nearer to the Objective [V] [TB1]: Attack In/Cv/Co/Ar [TB2]	
2	Move nearer to the Objective [V] [TB1]: Attack Co/In/Ar/Cv [TB2]
3	Move nearer to the Objective [H] [TB1]: Attack Co/In/Ar/Cv [TB2]
4-6	Move straight down: Attack Co/In/Ar/Cv [TB2]
Infantry (6)	**Set Up: Roll for Area; place on third or, if occupied, second hex down**
Attack nearest [Co/In/Cv/Ar] [TB2]	
1	Select nearest enemy [furthest up]. Move nearer to it [V] [TB1]: Attack nearest [Co/Ar/Cv/In] [TB2]
2-3	Move nearer to the Objective [V] [TB1]: Attack nearest [Co/Ar/Cv/In] [TB2]
4	Move nearer to the Objective [H] [TB1]: Attack nearest [Co/Ar/Cv/In] [TB2]
5-6	Move straight down: Attack nearest [Co/Ar/Cv/In] [TB2]
Commander: Sir Arthur Wellesley	**Set Up: Roll for Area 2,3,4; place on top hex**
Attack In/Cv/Co/Ar [TB2]	
If **T > 7** then Move nearer to the Objective [V] [TB1]: Attack In/Cv/Co/Ar [TB2]	
Select a vacant adjacent hex which is itself adjacent to *more* friendly units than the Commander is now [most friendly units] [furthest up] [TB1]. Move into it: Attack In/Cv/Co/Ar [TB2]	
Select the nearest *friendly* unit [In/Ar/Cv] [furthest up]. Move nearer to it [H] [TB1]: Attack In/Cv/Co/Ar [TB2]	

Unit	M	R	Units cannot Move if Square/engaged in battle	v Inf	v Cav	v Art
Infantry	1	3	Move or Square/De-Square, then Attack	4 - 3 - 2	3 - 2 - 2	3 - 2 - 2
Cavalry	2	1	Move, then Attack	6 - 5 - 4	4 - 3 - 2	4 - 3 - 2
Artillery	1	6	Move or Attack	3 - 2	2 - 1	2 - 1

Situation or Terrain (Units, High Ground & Buildings block LoS)	Dice	AI Tiebreaker Rules
Infantry attacking at *Range 1* after Moving	+1	**TB1: Move to which Hex?**
Infantry attacking *at Range 2-3* after Moving	-1	1. Within Range & LoS of enemy
Infantry attacking *at Range 2-3* whilst in Square formation	-1	2. Trees > Buildings hex
Infantry attacking Infantry who are in Square formation	+1	3. High Ground hex
Cavalry attacking Infantry who are in Square formation	-3	4. Hex not in a River
Artillery attacking at Range 1-3	+2	5. Hex Furthest Down
Artillery attacking Infantry who are in Square formation	+2	6. In/nearest to Area 3
Any unit attacking which is adjacent to its Commander	+1	**TB2: Attack which Enemy?**
Any unit attacking from Higher Ground than its Target	+1	1. Unit nearest Objective
Any unit attacking a unit in Trees or Buildings	-1	2. Unit Furthest Up
Any unit attacking through intervening Trees	-1	3. Unit not in Trees/Buildings
Any unit attacking from a River hex	-1	4. Strongest Unit

2. The Battle of Roliça, Part 1, 1808

3. The Battle of Roliça - Part 2, 17 August 1808 (British/Portuguese)

The French made a pre-planned retreat to a second position on higher ground to the south of Columbeira. **Objective:** *Destroy the French army entirely..*

Player: British & Portuguese		Place each Unit below the red dashed line	
Infantry: 5	Cavalry: 2	Artillery: 1	Commander: Sir Arthur Wellesley
Roll **3** dice. **Re-roll any dice once** (all together). **If Commander not KIA**, then 6s are Wild			

AI: French	Roll 4 dice. **Re-roll all duplicates under 6** (and all **6s** if Comm not KIA) once
Artillery (1)	Set Up: Roll for Area 1,2,3; place on fourth hex down

	Attack nearest [Ar/Co/In/Cv] [TB2]
5	Move horizontally downwards but only to put an enemy unit in Range *and* LoS [TB1]
6	Move straight down

Cavalry (1)	Set Up: Roll for Area 1,5; place on sixth hex down

	Attack Co/In/Ar/Cv [TB2]
2	Select nearest enemy [furthest up]. Move nearer to it [V] [TB1]: Attack In/Co/Ar/Cv [TB2]
3-6	If **T > 2** select nearest enemy [furthest up]. Move nearer to it [V] [TB1]: Attack In/Co/Ar/Cv [TB2]

Infantry (5)	Set Up: Place on second hex down of Areas 2,3,4,5 and top hex of Area 5

	If in Square & no enemy Cavalry within 3 hexes then De-Square: Attack nearest [Co/Ar/Cv/In] [TB2]
	If not in Square & enemy Cavalry are within 3 hexes then Square: Attack nearest [Co/Ar/Cv/In] [TB2]
	Attack nearest [Co/In/Cv/Ar] [TB2]
2-3	If not already on a High Ground hex, select an *adjacent* vacant High Ground hex [furthest down] [TB1]. Move onto it: Attack nearest [Co/Ar/Cv/In] [TB2]
4-5	Move straight down, but *only* if the destination hex is a High Ground hex: Attack nearest [Cv/In/Co/Ar] [TB2]
6	Move straight down: Attack nearest [Co/Ar/Cv/In] [TB2]

Commander: General Henri François Delaborde	Set Up: Roll for Area 2,3,4; place on top hex

	Attack In/Cv/Co/Ar [TB2]
1-2	If **T > 6** Move 1 hex straight up: Attack In/Cv/Co/Ar [TB2]
3-5	Select a vacant adjacent hex which is itself adjacent to *more* friendly units than the Commander is now [most friendly units] [furthest up] [TB1]. Move into it: Attack In/Cv/Co/Ar [TB2]
6	Select the nearest *friendly* unit [In/Ar/Cv] [furthest up]. Move nearer to it [H] [TB1]: Attack In/Cv/Co/Ar [TB2]

Unit	M	R	Units cannot Move if Square/engaged in battle	v Inf	v Cav	v Art
Infantry	1	3	Move or Square/De-Square, then Attack	4 - 3 - 2	3 - 2 - 2	3 - 2 - 2
Cavalry	2	1	Move, then Attack	6 - 5 - 4	4 - 3 - 2	4 - 3 - 2
Artillery	1	6	Move or Attack	3 - 2	2 - 1	2 - 1

Situation or Terrain (Units, High Ground & Buildings block LoS)	Dice	AI Tiebreaker Rules
Infantry attacking at *Range 1* after Moving	+1	**TB1: Move to which Hex?**
Infantry attacking *at Range 2-3* after Moving	-1	1. Within Range & LoS of enemy
Infantry attacking *at Range 2-3* whilst in Square formation	-1	2. Trees > Buildings hex
Infantry attacking Infantry who are in Square formation	+1	3. High Ground hex
Cavalry attacking Infantry who are in Square formation	-3	4. Hex not in a River
Artillery attacking at Range 1-3	+2	5. Hex Furthest Up
Artillery attacking Infantry who are in Square formation	+2	6. In/nearest to Area 3
Any unit attacking which is adjacent to its Commander	+1	**TB2: Attack which Enemy?**
Any unit attacking from Higher Ground than its Target	+1	1. Unit Furthest Up
Any unit attacking a unit in Trees or Buildings	-1	2. Unit not in Trees/Buildings
Any unit attacking through intervening Trees	-1	3. Strongest Unit
Any unit attacking from a River hex	-1	4. Unit nearest to Area 3

3. The Battle of Roliça, Part 2, 1808

Columbeira

Turn [1][2][3][4][5][6][7][8][9][10]

4. The Battle of Roliça - Part 2, 17 August 1808 (French)

The same Battle as the previous one, but this time you are the defending French army, vastly outnumbered as in the actual battle.

Objective: *Have at least three units remaining after 10 Turns.*

Player: French	Place each Unit below the blue dashed line		
Infantry: 3	Cavalry: 1	Artillery: 1	Commander: General Henri François Delaborde

Roll **3** dice. **Re-roll any dice once** (all together). **If** Commander **not KIA**, then 6s are Wild

AI: British/Portuguese	Roll **4** dice. **Re-roll all duplicates under 6** (and all **6s** if Comm not KIA) once
Artillery (1)	**Set Up: Roll for Area 3,4,5; place on fourth hex down**

Attack nearest [Ar/Co/In/Cv] [TB2]

1-3	Move horizontally downwards but only to put an enemy unit in Range *and* LoS [TB1]
4-6	Move straight down

Cavalry (4) Set Up:	**Place on third and fifth hexes down of Areas 4,5**

Attack Co/In/Ar/Cv [TB2]

2-5	Select nearest enemy [furthest up]. Move nearer to it [V] [TB1]: Attack Co/In/Ar/Cv [TB2]
6	Select nearest enemy [furthest up]. Move nearer to it [H] [TB1]: Attack Co/In/Ar/Cv [TB2]

Infantry (6)	**Set Up: Place on fifth and sixth hex down of Areas 1,2,3**

Attack nearest [Co/In/Cv/Ar] [TB2]

1-4	Select nearest enemy [furthest up]. Move nearer to it [V] [TB1]: Attack nearest [Co/Ar/Cv/In] [TB2]
5	Move horizontally down to the right: Attack nearest [Cv/Co/In/Ar] [TB2]
6	Move straight down: Attack nearest [Co/Ar/Cv/In] [TB2]

Commander: Sir Arthur Wellesley	**Set Up: Roll for Area 1,2,3; place on third hex down**

Attack In/Cv/Co/Ar [TB2]

If **T > 6** then select nearest enemy [furthest up]. Move nearer to it [V] [TB1]: Attack In/Cv/Co/Ar [TB2]

Select a vacant adjacent hex which is itself adjacent to *more* friendly units than the Commander is now [most friendly units] [furthest up] [TB1]. Move into it: Attack In/Cv/Co/Ar [TB2]

Select the nearest *friendly* unit [In/Ar/Cv]. Move nearer to it [H] [TB1]: Attack In/Cv/Co/Ar [TB2]

Unit	M	R	Units cannot Move if Square/engaged in battle	v Inf	v Cav	v Art
Infantry	1	3	Move or Square/De-Square, then Attack	4 - 3 - 2	3 - 2 - 2	3 - 2 - 2
Cavalry	2	1	Move, then Attack	6 - 5 - 4	4 - 3 - 2	4 - 3 - 2
Artillery	1	6	Move or Attack	3 - 2	2 - 1	2 - 1

Situation or Terrain (Units, High Ground & Buildings block LoS)	Dice	AI Tiebreaker Rules	
Infantry attacking **at *Range 1* after Moving**	**+1**	**TB1: Move to which Hex?**	
Infantry attacking ***at Range 2-3* after Moving**	**-1**	1. Within Range & LoS of enemy	
Infantry attacking ***at Range 2-3* whilst in Square formation**	**-1**	2. Trees > Buildings hex	
Infantry attacking Infantry **who are in Square formation**	**+1**	3. High Ground hex	
Cavalry attacking Infantry **who are in Square formation**	**-3**	4. Hex not in a River	
Artillery attacking **at Range 1-3**	**+2**	5. Hex Furthest Down	
Artillery attacking Infantry **who are in Square formation**	**+2**	6. In/nearest to Area 3	
Any unit attacking **which is adjacent to its** Commander	**+1**	**TB2: Attack which Enemy?**	
Any unit attacking **from Higher Ground than its Target**	**+1**	1. Unit Furthest Up	
Any unit attacking **a unit in Trees or Buildings**	**-1**	2. Unit not in Trees/Buildings	
Any unit attacking **through intervening Trees**	**-1**	3. Strongest Unit	
Any unit attacking **from a River hex**	**-1**	4. Unit nearest to Area 3	

4. The Battle of Roliça, Part 2, 1808

Columbeira

Turn [1][2][3][4][5][6][7][8][9][10]

5. The Battle of Vimeiro, 21 August 1808 (British/Portuguese)

Having defeated the French at Roliça, Sir Arthur Wellesley planned to advance on and attack Marshal Junot's French army. Although confident of victory, he had concerns over the stronger French Cavalry.

Objective: *Occupy the town of **Vimeiro** with any unit <u>at the end</u> of Turn 10.*

Player: British & Portuguese		Place each Unit below the red dashed line	
Infantry: 4	Cavalry: 1	Artillery: 1	Commander: Sir Arthur Wellesley
Roll 3 dice. **Re-roll any dice once** (all together). **If Commander not KIA**, then 6s are Wild			

AI: French	Roll **4 dice**. **Re-roll all duplicates under 6** (and all **6s if Comm not KIA**) once
Artillery (1)	**Set Up: Place on second hex down of Area 4**
Attack nearest [Ar/Co/In/Cv] [TB2]	
4-5	Move horizontally downwards but only to put an enemy unit in Range *and* LoS [TB1]
6	Move straight down
Cavalry (2)	**Set Up: Roll for Area 1,2,3,5; place on fourth hex down**
Attack Co/In/Ar/Cv [TB2]	
1-2	If any enemy is within 3 hexes then select the nearest enemy [nearest to Vimeiro] [furthest up]. Move nearer to it [V] [TB1]: Attack In/Cv/Co/Ar [TB2]
3-4	Select nearest enemy [furthest up]. Move nearer to it [V] [TB1]: Attack Co/In/Ar/Cv [TB2]
5-6	If T > 5 Move nearer to Vimeiro [V] [TB1]: Attack Co/In/Ar/Cv [TB2]
Infantry (8) Set Up: Place on second hex down of Areas 2,3,5 and third hex down of Areas 1,2,3,4,5	
If in Square & no enemy Cavalry within 3 hexes then De-Square: Attack nearest [Co/Ar/Cv/In] [TB2]	
If *on* the Vimeiro hex and not in Square and enemy Cavalry are within 3 hexes then Square: Attack nearest [Co/Ar/Cv/In] [TB2]	
Attack nearest [Co/In/Cv/Ar] [TB2]	
1-2	If Vimeiro is vacant Move nearer to it [V] [TB1]: Attack nearest [Co/Ar/Cv/In] [TB2]
3-4	Move straight down, but *not* if it results in the unit Moving from a High Ground hex to a non-High Ground hex: Attack nearest [Co/Ar/Cv/In] [TB2]
5-6	Select nearest enemy [furthest up]. Move nearer to it [H] [TB1]: Attack nearest [Co/Ar/Cv/In] [TB2]
Commander: Marshal Junot	**Set Up: Roll for Area 2,3,4; place on top hex**
Attack In/Cv/Co/Ar [TB2]	
If T > 5 and Vimeiro is vacant Move nearer to it [H] [TB1]: Attack In/Cv/Co/Ar [TB2]	
Select a vacant adjacent hex which is itself adjacent to *more* friendly units than the Commander is now [most friendly units] [furthest up] [TB1]. Move into it: Attack In/Cv/Co/Ar [TB2]	

Unit	M	R	Units cannot Move if Square/engaged in battle	v Inf	v Cav	v Art
Infantry	1	3	Move or Square/De-Square, then Attack	4 - 3 - 2	3 - 2 - 2	3 - 2 - 2
Cavalry	2	1	Move, then Attack	6 - 5 - 4	4 - 3 - 2	4 - 3 - 2
Artillery	1	6	Move or Attack	3 - 2	2 - 1	2 - 1

Situation or Terrain (Units, High Ground & Buildings block LoS)	Dice	AI Tiebreaker Rules	
Infantry attacking **at Range 1 after Moving**	+1	**TB1: Move to which Hex?**	
Infantry attacking *at Range 2-3 after Moving*	-1	1. Within Range & LoS of enemy	
Infantry attacking *at Range 2-3 whilst in Square formation*	-1	2. Trees > Buildings hex	
Infantry attacking Infantry **who are in Square formation**	+1	3. High Ground hex	
Cavalry attacking Infantry **who are in Square formation**	-3	4. Hex not in a River	
Artillery attacking **at Range 1-3**	+2	5. Hex Furthest Up	
Artillery attacking Infantry **who are in Square formation**	+2	6. Nearest to Vimeiro	
Any unit attacking **which is adjacent to its Commander**	+1	**TB2: Attack which Enemy?**	
Any unit attacking **from Higher Ground than its Target**	+1	1. Unit nearest to Vimeiro	
Any unit attacking **a unit in Trees or Buildings**	-1	2. Unit Furthest Up	
Any unit attacking **through intervening Trees**	-1	3. Unit not in Trees/Buildings	
Any unit attacking **from a River hex**	-1	4. Strongest Unit	

5. The Battle of Vimeiro, 1808

Maceira

Vimeiro

Turn [1][2][3][4][5][6][7][8][9][10]

6. The Battle of Vimeiro, 21 August 1808 (French)

The same Battle again but from the French point of view. Marshal Junot had also planned to advance and attack the British and Portuguese army. He assembled his army at Torres Vedras and marched towards Vimeiro.

Objective: *Occupy the town of **Vimeiro** with any unit <u>at the end</u> of Turn 10.*

Player: French	Place each Unit below the blue dashed line		
Infantry: 4	Cavalry: 1	Artillery: 1	Commander: Marshal Junot
Roll **3** dice. **Re-roll any dice once** (all together). **If Commander not KIA**, then 6s are Wild			

AI: British/Portuguese	Roll 4 dice. **Re-roll all duplicates under 6** (and all **6s** if Comm not KIA) once
Artillery (1)	**Set Up: Roll for Area 2,3; place on top hex**
Attack nearest [Ar/Co/In/Cv] [TB2]	
3-4	Move horizontally downwards but only to put an enemy unit in Range *and* LoS [TB1]
5-6	Move straight down
Cavalry (2)	**Set Up: Roll for Area; place on third hex down**
Attack Co/In/Ar/Cv [TB2]	
1-2	If any enemy is within 3 hexes then select the nearest enemy [nearest to Vimeiro] [furthest up]. Move nearer to it [V] [TB1]: Attack In/Cv/Co/Ar [TB2]
3-4	Select nearest enemy [furthest up]. Move nearer to it [V] [TB1]: Attack Co/In/Ar/Cv [TB2]
5-6	If **T > 5** Move nearer to Vimeiro [V] [TB1]: Attack Co/In/Ar/Cv [TB2]
Infantry (7)	**Set Up: Place on second hex down of Areas 1,2,3,4,5 and fourth hex down of Area 1,4**
If in Square & no enemy Cavalry within 3 hexes then De-Square: Attack nearest [Co/Ar/Cv/In] [TB2]	
If *on* the Vimeiro hex and not in Square and enemy Cavalry are within 3 hexes then Square: Attack nearest [Co/Ar/Cv/In] [TB2]	
Attack nearest [Co/In/Cv/Ar] [TB2]	
1-2	If Vimeiro is vacant Move nearer to it [V] [TB1]: Attack nearest [Co/Ar/Cv/In] [TB2]
3-4	Move straight down: Attack nearest [Co/Ar/Cv/In] [TB2]
5-6	Select nearest enemy [furthest up]. Move nearer to it [H][TB1]: Attack nearest [Co/Ar/Cv/In] [TB2]
Commander: Sir Arthur Wellesley	**Set Up: Place on top hex of Area 4**
Attack In/Cv/Co/Ar [TB2]	
If **T > 5** and Vimeiro is vacant Move nearer to it [H] [TB1]: Attack In/Cv/Co/Ar [TB2]	
Select a vacant adjacent hex which is itself adjacent to *more* friendly units than the Commander is now [most friendly units] [furthest up] [TB1]. Move into it: Attack In/Cv/Co/Ar [TB2]	

Unit	M	R	Units cannot Move if Square/engaged in battle	v Inf	v Cav	v Art
Infantry	1	3	Move or Square/De-Square, then Attack	4 - 3 - 2	3 - 2 - 2	3 - 2 - 2
Cavalry	2	1	Move, then Attack	6 - 5 - 4	4 - 3 - 2	4 - 3 - 2
Artillery	1	6	Move or Attack	3 - 2	2 - 1	2 - 1

Situation or Terrain (Units, High Ground & Buildings block LoS)	Dice	AI Tiebreaker Rules
Infantry attacking **at Range 1 after Moving**	+1	**TB1: Move to which Hex?**
Infantry attacking **at Range 2-3 after Moving**	-1	1. Within Range & LoS of enemy
Infantry attacking **at Range 2-3 whilst in Square formation**	-1	2. Trees > Buildings hex
Infantry attacking Infantry **who are in Square formation**	+1	3. High Ground hex
Cavalry attacking Infantry **who are in Square formation**	-3	4. Hex not in a River
Artillery attacking **at Range 1-3**	+2	5. Hex Furthest Down
Artillery attacking Infantry **who are in Square formation**	+2	6. Nearest to Vimeiro
Any unit attacking **which is adjacent to its Commander**	+1	**TB2: Attack which Enemy?**
Any unit attacking **from Higher Ground than its Target**	+1	1. Unit nearest to Vimeiro
Any unit attacking **a unit in Trees or Buildings**	-1	2. Unit Furthest Up
Any unit attacking **through intervening Trees**	-1	3. Unit not in Trees/Buildings
Any unit attacking **from a River hex**	-1	4. Strongest Unit

6. The Battle of Vimeiro, 1808

7. The Battle of Sahagun, 21 December 1808 (British)

Heading to Madrid to assist the Spanish, Major-General Paget marched to Sahagun in northern Spain to face a French Cavalry brigade which was lodging at a nearby monastery. The exact numbers involved in this small Battle are not certain, but the British Cavalry defeated the French.

Objective: *Eliminate the French army.*

Player: British		Place each Unit below the red dashed line	
Infantry: 0	Cavalry: 3	Artillery: 1	Commander: Major-General Lord Henry Paget
Roll 3 dice. **Re-roll any dice once** (all together). **If Commander not KIA**, then 6s are Wild			

AI: French	Roll 4 dice. **Re-roll all duplicates under 6** (and all **6s** if Comm not KIA) once
Artillery (0)	Set Up: Not applicable
Cavalry (4)	Set Up: Roll for Area; place on top hex or, if occupied, second hex down

Attack Co/Ar/Cv [TB2]	
1-3	If any enemy is within 3 hexes then select the nearest enemy [furthest up] [strongest]. Move nearer to it [V] [TB1]: Attack Cv/Co/Ar [TB2]
4	Move straight down *one hex only*: Attack Co/Ar/Cv [TB2]
5-6	If Turn **<7** select nearest <u>friendly</u> unit [Co/Cv] [furthest down]. Move nearer to it [H] [TB1]: Attack Cv/Co/Ar [TB2] If **T > 6** select nearest High Ground hex [furthest up]. Move nearer to it [V] [TB1]: Attack Cv/Co/Ar [TB2]

Infantry (0)	Set Up: Not applicable
Commander: General Debelle	Set Up: Roll for Area; place on top hex
Attack Cv/Co/Ar [TB2]	
If **T > 6** select nearest High Ground hex [adjacent to most friendly units] [furthest up]. Move nearer to it [V] [TB1]: Attack Cv/Co/Ar [TB2]	
Select a vacant adjacent hex which is itself adjacent to *more* friendly units than the Commander is now [most friendly units] [furthest up] [TB1]. Move into it: Attack Cv/Co/Ar [TB2]	

Unit	M	R	Units cannot Move if Square/engaged in battle	v Inf	v Cav	v Art
Infantry	1	3	Move or Square/De-Square, then Attack	4 - 3 - 2	3 - 2 - 2	3 - 2 - 2
Cavalry	2	1	Move, then Attack	6 - 5 - 4	4 - 3 - 2	4 - 3 - 2
Artillery	1	6	Move or Attack	3 - 2	2 - 1	2 - 1

Situation or Terrain (Units, High Ground & Buildings block LoS)	Dice	AI Tiebreaker Rules
Infantry attacking *at Range 1 after Moving*	+1	**TB1: Move to which Hex?**
Infantry attacking *at Range 2-3 after Moving*	-1	1. Within Range & LoS of enemy
Infantry attacking *at Range 2-3 whilst in Square formation*	-1	2. Trees > Buildings hex
Infantry attacking Infantry who are in Square formation	+1	3. High Ground hex
Cavalry attacking Infantry who are in Square formation	-3	4. Hex not in a River
Artillery attacking at Range 1-3	+2	5. Hex Furthest Up
Artillery attacking Infantry who are in Square formation	+2	6. In/nearest to Area 3
Any unit attacking which is adjacent to its Commander	+1	**TB2: Attack which Enemy?**
Any unit attacking from Higher Ground than its Target	+1	1. Unit Furthest Up
Any unit attacking a unit in Trees or Buildings	-1	2. Unit not in Trees/Buildings
Any unit attacking through intervening Trees	-1	3. Strongest Unit
Any unit attacking from a River hex	-1	4. Unit nearest to Area 3

7. The Battle of Sahagun, 1808

Sahagun

8. The Battle of Sahagun, 21 December 1808 (French)

The same Battle as the previous Battle, but this time your task is to help the French resist the British advance and to push them back.

Objective: *Push all British units back above the red dashed line <u>at any point from the beginning of Turn 5 onwards.</u>*

Player: French	Place each Unit below the blue dashed line		
Infantry: 0	Cavalry: 3	Artillery: 0	Commander: General Debelle
Roll 3 dice. **Re-roll any dice once** (all together). If Commander **not KIA**, then 6s are Wild			

AI: British	Roll **4 dice. Re-roll all duplicates under 6** (and all **6s** if Comm not KIA) once
Artillery (1)	
Set Up: Roll for Area 3,4,5; place on third hex down	
Attack nearest [Co/Cv] [TB2]	
1-2	If positioned *above* the red dashed line then Move vertically straight down
3-4	Move horizontally downward to the left
5-6	Move straight down
Cavalry (4)	**Set Up: Roll for Area; place on second or, if occupied, third hex down**
Attack Co/Cv [TB2]	
1-2	If any enemy is within 3 hexes, then select the nearest enemy [furthest up] [strongest]. Move nearer to it [V] [TB1]: Attack Cv/Co [TB2]
3-4	Select nearest enemy [furthest up] [strongest]. Move nearer to it [V] [TB1]: Attack Co/Cv [TB2]
5-6	Select nearest enemy [strongest] [furthest up]. Move nearer to it [H] [TB1]: Attack Co/Cv [TB2]
Infantry (0)	**Set Up: Not Applicable**
Commander: Major-General Lord Henry Paget	**Set Up: Roll for Area; Place on top hex**
Attack Cv/Co [TB2]	
Select a vacant adjacent hex which is itself adjacent to *more* friendly units than the Commander is now [most friendly units] [furthest up] [TB1]. Move into it: Attack Co/Cv [TB2]	
Select nearest *friendly* unit [Cv/Ar] [furthest up]. Move nearer to it [H] [TB1]: Attack Cv/Co [TB2]	

Unit	M	R	Units cannot Move if Square/engaged in battle	v Inf	v Cav	v Art
Infantry	1	3	Move or Square/De-Square, then Attack	4 - 3 - 2	3 - 2 - 2	3 - 2 - 2
Cavalry	2	1	Move, then Attack	6 - 5 - 4	4 - 3 - 2	4 - 3 - 2
Artillery	1	6	Move or Attack	3 - 2	2 - 1	2 - 1

Situation or Terrain (Units, High Ground & Buildings block LoS)	Dice	AI Tiebreaker Rules
Infantry attacking **at *Range 1* after Moving**	+1	**TB1: Move to which Hex?**
Infantry attacking **at *Range 2-3* after Moving**	-1	1. Within Range & LoS of enemy
Infantry attacking **at *Range 2-3* whilst in Square formation**	-1	2. Trees > Buildings hex
Infantry attacking Infantry **who are in Square formation**	+1	3. High Ground hex
Cavalry attacking Infantry **who are in Square formation**	-3	4. Hex not in a River
Artillery attacking **at Range 1-3**	+2	5. Hex Furthest Down
Artillery attacking Infantry **who are in Square formation**	+2	6. In/nearest to Area 3
Any unit attacking **which is adjacent to its** Commander	+1	**TB2: Attack which Enemy?**
Any unit attacking **from Higher Ground than its Target**	+1	1. Unit Furthest Up
Any unit attacking **a unit in Trees or Buildings**	-1	2. Unit not in Trees/Buildings
Any unit attacking **through intervening Trees**	-1	3. Strongest Unit
Any unit attacking **from a River hex**	-1	4. Unit nearest to Area 3

8. The Battle of Sahagun, 1808

Sahagun

9. The Battle of Cacabelos, 3 January 1809 (British)

The British army was retreating to the north-west of Spain towards Corunna, pursued by a stronger French army. The British rear guard successfully repelled the French attackers, enabling the retreat.

Objective: *Prevent any French unit exiting the bottom of the Battle Map at any point in the game. It will do this if its 'Move straight down' instruction requires it to Move to a hex below the Map.*

Player: British & Portuguese		Place each Unit within the red dashed outlined area	
Infantry: 4	Cavalry: 1	Artillery: 1	Commander: General Edward Paget
Roll 3 dice. **Re-roll any dice once** (all together). If Commander **not KIA**, then 6s are Wild			

AI: French	Roll 4 dice. **Re-roll all duplicates under 6** (and all **6s** if Comm not KIA) once
Artillery (0)	Set Up: Not Applicable
Cavalry (4)	Set Up: Roll for Area; place on top hex or second hex down

Attack Co/In/Ar/Cv [TB2]

1-3	If **T>2** Move straight down: Attack In/Cv/Co/Ar [TB2]
4-6	Select nearest enemy unit [furthest down]. Move nearer to it [V][TB1]: Attack Co/In/Ar/Cv [TB2]

Infantry (5)	Set Up: Roll for Area; place on third, fourth or fifth hex down

Attack nearest [Co/In/Cv/Ar] [TB2]

1-3	Move straight down: Attack nearest [Co/Ar/Cv/In] [TB2]
4-5	Select nearest enemy unit [furthest up]. Move nearer to it [V] [TB1]: Attack nearest [Co/Ar/Cv/In] [TB2]
6	Select nearest enemy unit [furthest up]. Move nearer to it [H] [TB1]: Attack nearest [In/Co/Ar/Cv] [TB2]

Commander: General Colbert	Set Up: Roll for Area; place on top hex

Attack In/Cv/Co/Ar [TB2]

If **T > 6** Move straight down: Attack In/Cv/Co/Ar [TB2]

If **T > 6** Move *one hex* horizontally down to the left: Attack In/Cv/Co/Ar [TB2]

If **T > 6** Move *one hex* horizontally down to the right: Attack In/Cv/Co/Ar [TB2]

Select a vacant adjacent hex which is itself adjacent to *more* friendly units than the Commander is now [most friendly units] [furthest up] [TB1]. Move into it: Attack In/Cv/Co/Ar [TB2]

If not adjacent to any friendly unit, select nearest *friendly Infantry* unit [furthest up]. Move nearer to it [H] [TB1]: Attack Cv/Co [TB2]

Unit	M	R	Units cannot Move if Square/engaged in battle	v Inf	v Cav	v Art
Infantry	1	3	Move or Square/De-Square, then Attack	4 - 3 - 2	3 - 2 - 2	3 - 2 - 2
Cavalry	2	1	Move, then Attack	6 - 5 - 4	4 - 3 - 2	4 - 3 - 2
Artillery	1	6	Move or Attack	3 - 2	2 - 1	2 - 1

Situation or Terrain (Units, High Ground & Buildings block LoS)	Dice	AI Tiebreaker Rules
Infantry attacking **at *Range 1* after Moving**	+1	**TB1: Move to which Hex?**
Infantry attacking **at *Range 2-3* after Moving**	-1	1. Within Range & LoS of enemy
Infantry attacking **at *Range 2-3* whilst in Square formation**	-1	2. Trees > Buildings hex
Infantry attacking Infantry **who are in Square formation**	+1	3. High Ground hex
Cavalry attacking Infantry **who are in Square formation**	-3	4. Hex not in a River
Artillery attacking **at Range 1-3**	+2	5. Hex Furthest Down
Artillery attacking Infantry **who are in Square formation**	+2	6. In/nearest to Area 3
Any unit attacking **which is adjacent to its** Commander	+1	**TB2: Attack which Enemy?**
Any unit attacking **from Higher Ground than its Target**	+1	1. Unit Furthest Up
Any unit attacking **a unit in Trees or Buildings**	-1	2. Unit not in Trees/Buildings
Any unit attacking **through intervening Trees**	-1	3. Strongest Unit
Any unit attacking **from a River hex**	-1	4. Unit nearest to Area 3

10. The Battle of Cacabelos, 3 January 1809 (French)

The same Battle but this time you play as the French trying to chase down the main British army beyond the rear guard. **Objective:** *Move any French unit off the top of the Battle Map.*

Player: French		Place each Unit below the blue dashed line	
Infantry: 4	Cavalry: 2	Artillery: 0	Commander: General Colbert
Roll **3** dice. **Re-roll any dice once** (all together). **If** Commander **not KIA**, then 6s are Wild			

AI: British	Roll **4** dice. **Re-roll all duplicates under 6** (and all **6s** if Comm **not KIA**) once
Artillery (1)	**Set Up: Roll for Area; place on top hex**

	Attack nearest [Co/In/Cv] [TB2]
1-2	Move, but only to an adjacent High Ground hex [TB1]
3-6	Move left or right *along the top row of hexes only* but only to put an enemy unit in Range *and* LoS [TB1]

Cavalry (3) Set Up: Roll for Area (but re-roll if it is the same Area as the Artillery); place on third hex down	
Attack In/Co/Cv [TB2]	
Select nearest enemy in a hex upwards of the River (i.e., that has *crossed/passed* the River) [furthest up] [Cv/Co/In]. Move nearer to it [H] [TB1]: Attack Cv/Co/In [TB2]	
1-4	If any enemy is within 3 hexes, then select the nearest enemy [furthest up] [strongest]. Move nearer to it [V] [TB1]: Attack Cv/In/Co [TB2]
5-6	Select nearest enemy unit [furthest up]. Move nearer to it [H] [TB1]: Attack Cv/In/Co [TB2]

Infantry (7) Set Up: Place on seventh hex down of every Area and eighth hex down of 2 random Areas	
If on a High Ground hex *and* not in Square *and* enemy Cavalry are within 3 hexes then Square: Attack nearest [Co/Cv/In] [TB2] (*unit will remain in Square for the rest of the game*)	
Attack nearest [Cv/In/Co] [TB2]	
1-3	Move straight *up*: Attack nearest [Co/Cv/In] [TB2]
4-6	Select nearest enemy [furthest up]. Move nearer to it [H][TB1]: Attack nearest [Cv/Co/In] [TB2]

Commander: General Edward Paget	**Set Up: Roll for Area 2,3,4; place on second hex down**
Attack In/Cv/Co	
Select nearest enemy in a hex upwards of the River (i.e., that has *crossed/passed* the River) [furthest up] [Cv/Co/In]. Move nearer to it [H] [TB1]: Attack Cv/Co/In [TB2]	
If any enemy is within 3 hexes, then select the nearest enemy [furthest up] [weakest]. Move nearer to it [V] [TB1]: Attack Cv/In/Co [TB2]	
3-4	Move down to the left: Attack Cv/In/Co [TB2]
5-6	Move down to the right: Attack Cv/In/Co [TB2]

Unit	M	R	Units cannot Move if Square/engaged in battle	v Inf	v Cav	v Art
Infantry	1	3	Move or Square/De-Square, then Attack	4 - 3 - 2	3 - 2 - 2	3 - 2 - 2
Cavalry	2	1	Move, then Attack	6 - 5 - 4	4 - 3 - 2	4 - 3 - 2
Artillery	1	6	Move or Attack	3 - 2	2 - 1	2 - 1

Situation or Terrain (Units, High Ground & Buildings block LoS)	Dice	AI Tiebreaker Rules	
Infantry attacking *at Range 1* after Moving	+1	**TB1: Move to which Hex?**	
Infantry attacking *at Range 2-3* after Moving	-1	1. Within Range & LoS of enemy	
Infantry attacking *at Range 2-3* whilst in Square formation	-1	2. Trees > Buildings hex	
Infantry attacking Infantry who are in Square formation	+1	3. High Ground hex	
Cavalry attacking Infantry who are in Square formation	-3	4. Hex not in a River	
Artillery attacking **at Range 1-3**	+2	5. Hex Furthest Up	
Artillery attacking Infantry who are in Square formation	+2	6. In/nearest to Area 3	
Any unit attacking **which is adjacent to its** Commander	+1	**TB2: Attack which Enemy?**	
Any unit attacking **from Higher Ground than its Target**	+1	1. Unit Furthest Up	
Any unit attacking **a unit in Trees or Buildings**	-1	2. Unit not in Trees/Buildings	
Any unit attacking **through intervening Trees**	-1	3. Strongest Unit	
Any unit attacking **from a River hex**	-1	4. Unit nearest to Area 3	

10. The Battle of Cacabelos, 1809

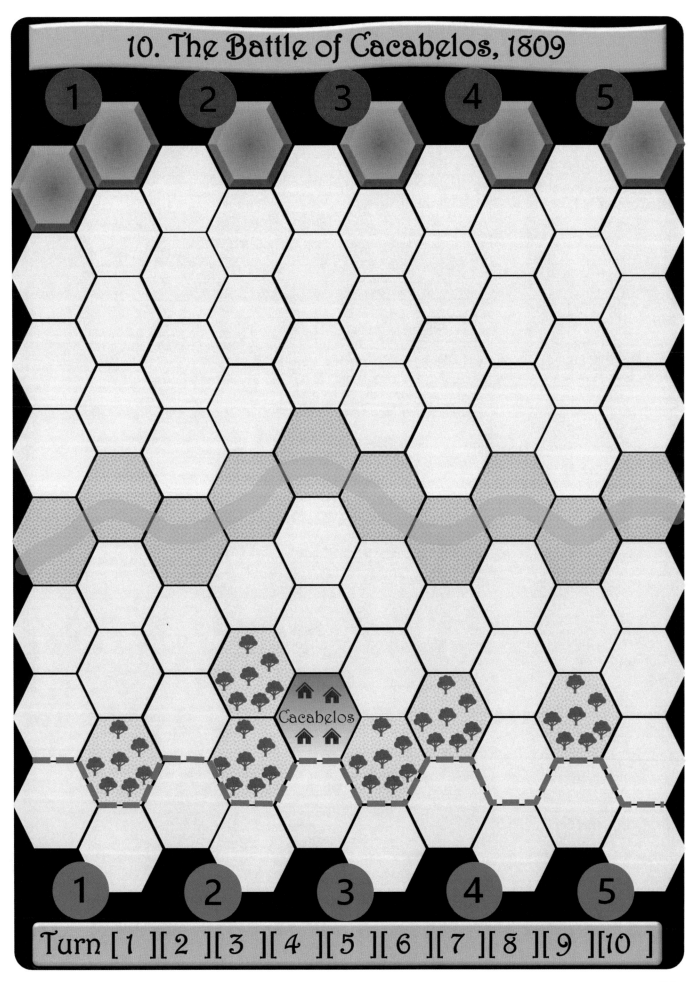

Cacabelos

11. The Battle of Corunna, 16 January 1809 (British)

Having defeated the Spanish army, Napoleon was coming after Sir John Moore's British army, which needed to retreat to Corunna for evacuation by the Royal Navy. Although successful in the retreat, Sir John Moore was fatally wounded in the Battle.

Objective: *Keep the British Commander, Sir John Moore, alive until the end of the Battle.*

Player: British	Place each Unit within the red dashed outlined area		
Infantry: 5	Cavalry: 0	Artillery: 1	Commander: Sir John Moore
Roll **3** dice. **Re-roll any dice once** (all together). **If Commander not KIA**, then 6s are Wild			

AI: French	Roll **4** dice. **Re-roll all duplicates under 6** (and all **6s** if Comm not KIA) once
Artillery (1)	**Set Up: Roll for Area 1,4,5; place on top hex**

Attack nearest [Co/Ar/In] [TB2]	
1-2	Move horizontally downwards but only to put an enemy unit in Range *and* LoS [TB1]
3-6	Move straight down

Cavalry (2)	**Set Up: Place on fourth hex down of Area 1 and third hex down of Area 5**
Attack Co/In/Ar [TB2]	
If **T > 7** Move nearer to the British Commander [H] [TB1]: Attack Co/In/Ar [TB2]	
1-2	If any enemy is within 3 hexes then select the nearest enemy [nearest to British Commander] [furthest up]. Move nearer to it [H] [TB1]: Attack Co/In/Ar [TB2]
3-4	Select nearest enemy [furthest up]. Move nearer to it [V] [TB1]: Attack Co/In/Ar [TB2]
5-6	Move nearer to the British Commander [V] [TB1]: Attack Co/In/Ar [TB2]

Infantry (8) Set Up: Place on fourth hex down of Areas 2,3,4,5 and fifth hex down of Areas 1,2,3,4	
Attack nearest [Co/In/Ar] [TB2]	
If **T > 5** Move nearer to the *British* Commander [V] [TB1]: Attack nearest Co/In/Ar [TB2]	
1	Move downwards to the left: Attack nearest [Co/Ar/In] [TB2]
2	Move downwards to the right: Attack nearest [Co/In/Ar] [TB2]
3-6	Move straight down: Attack nearest [Co/Ar/In] [TB2]

Commander: Marshal Soult	**Set Up: Roll for Area 2,3; place on second hex down**
Attack Co/In/Ar [TB2]	
If **T > 6** Move nearer to the British Commander [H] [TB1]: Attack Co/In/Ar [TB2]	
Select a vacant adjacent hex which is itself adjacent to *more* friendly units than the Commander is now [most friendly units] [furthest up] [TB1]. Move into it: Attack Co/In/Ar [TB2]	

Unit	M	R	Units cannot Move if Square/engaged in battle	v Inf	v Cav	v Art
Infantry	1	3	Move or Square/De-Square, then Attack	4 - 3 - 2	3 - 2 - 2	3 - 2 - 2
Cavalry	2	1	Move, then Attack	6 - 5 - 4	4 - 3 - 2	4 - 3 - 2
Artillery	1	6	Move or Attack	3 - 2	2 - 1	2 - 1

Situation or Terrain (Units, High Ground & Buildings block LoS)	Dice	AI Tiebreaker Rules
Infantry attacking *at Range 1* after Moving	+1	**TB1: Move to which Hex?**
Infantry attacking *at Range 2-3* after Moving	-1	1. Within Range & LoS of enemy
Infantry attacking *at Range 2-3* whilst in Square formation	-1	2. Trees > Buildings hex
Infantry attacking Infantry who are in Square formation	+1	3. High Ground hex
Cavalry attacking Infantry who are in Square formation	-3	4. Hex not in a River
Artillery attacking at Range 1-3	+2	5. Hex Furthest Down
Artillery attacking Infantry who are in Square formation	+2	6. Hex nearest British Commander
Any unit attacking which is adjacent to its Commander	+1	**TB2: Attack which Enemy?**
Any unit attacking from Higher Ground than its Target	+1	1. Unit nearest British Commander
Any unit attacking a unit in Trees or Buildings	-1	2. Unit Furthest Up
Any unit attacking through intervening Trees	-1	3. Unit not in Trees/Buildings
Any unit attacking from a River hex	-1	4. Strongest Unit

11. The Battle of Corunna, 1809

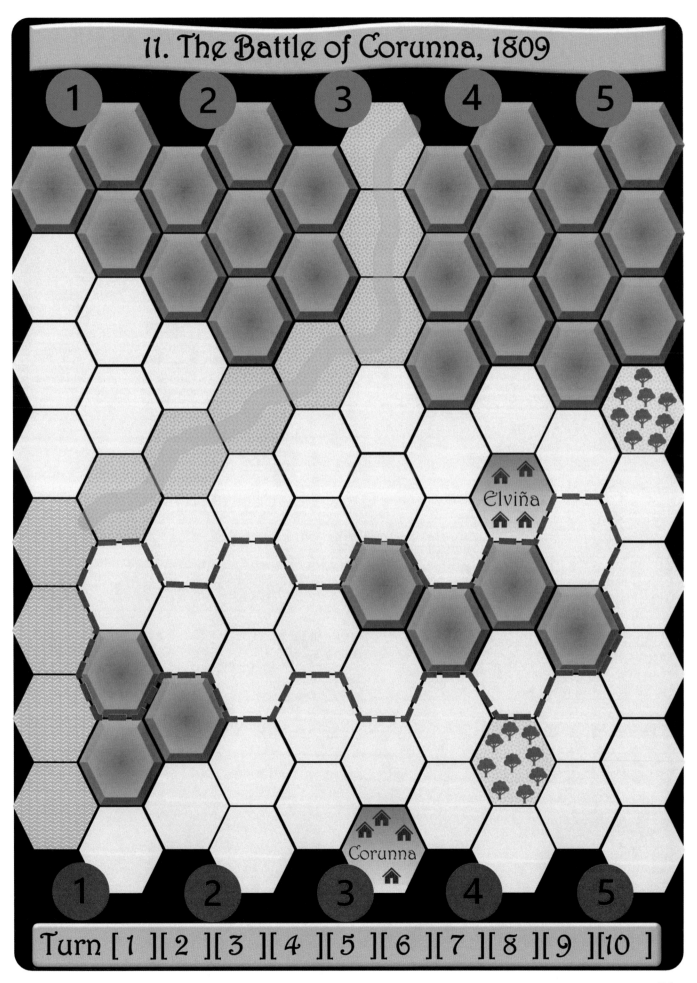

12. The Battle of Corunna, 16 January 1809 (French)

This time your task is to defeat the British defence and kill their Commander.

Objective: *Kill the British Commander, Sir John Moore, before the end of the Battle.*

Player: French	Place each Unit below the blue dashed line		
Infantry: 5	Cavalry: 1	Artillery: 1	Commander: Marshal Soult
Roll **3** dice. **Re-roll any dice once** (all together). **If Commander not KIA**, then 6s are Wild			

AI: British	Roll **4** dice. **Re-roll all duplicates under 6** (and all **6s if Comm not KIA**) once
Artillery (1)	**Set Up: Place randomly on one of the hexes marked 'A'**
Attack nearest [Ar/Co/In/Cv] [TB2]	
1-2	If not currently on a Higher Ground hex, Move straight down
3-6	Move to an adjacent Higher Ground hex but only to put an enemy unit in Range *and* LoS [TB1]
Cavalry (0)	**Set Up: Not Applicable**
Infantry (7)	**Set Up: Roll for Area 1,2,3,4; place on third or, if occupied, fifth hex down**
If in Square & no enemy Cavalry within 3 hexes then De-Square: Attack nearest [Co/Ar/Cv/In] [TB2]	
If not in Square and enemy Cavalry are within 3 hexes then Square: Attack nearest [Cv/Co/Ar/In] [TB2]	
Attack nearest [Cv/In/Co/Ar] [TB2]	
If **T > 5** then Move nearer to the British Commander [V] [TB1]: Attack nearest Cv/Co/In/Ar [TB2]	
2-3	If not already on a High Ground hex, select an *adjacent* vacant High Ground hex [nearest to British Commander] [furthest down] [TB1]. Move onto it: Attack nearest [Cv/In/Co/Ar] [TB2]
4	Move straight *up*: Attack nearest [Cv/Co/In/Ar] [TB2]
5-6	Select nearest enemy [furthest up]. Move nearer to it [H][TB1]: Attack nearest [Co/Ar/Cv/In] [TB2]
Commander: Sir John Moore	
Set Up: Roll for Area 2,3; place on second hex down	
Attack In/Cv/Co/Ar [TB2]	
If Commander is in Range and LoS of any French unit, select an adjacent hex which is not [furthest up] [TB1]. Move onto it: Attack In/Cv/Co/Ar [TB2]	
If **T > 4** Move nearer to Corunna [H] [TB1]: Attack In/Cv/Co/Ar [TB2]	
1-2	If **T < 5** Move straight *up*: Attack In/Cv/Co/Ar [TB2]
3-6	If **T < 5** Select a vacant adjacent hex which is *not* a Higher Ground hex and which is itself adjacent to *more* friendly units than the Commander is now [most friendly units] [furthest up] [TB1]. Move into it: Attack In/Cv/Co/Ar [TB2]

Unit	M	R	Units cannot Move if Square/engaged in battle	v Inf	v Cav	v Art
Infantry	1	3	Move or Square/De-Square, then Attack	4 - 3 - 2	3 - 2 - 2	3 - 2 - 2
Cavalry	2	1	Move, then Attack	6 - 5 - 4	4 - 3 - 2	4 - 3 - 2
Artillery	1	6	Move or Attack	3 - 2	2 - 1	2 - 1

Situation or Terrain (Units, High Ground & Buildings block LoS)	Dice	AI Tiebreaker Rules
Infantry attacking **at Range 1 after Moving**	+1	**TB1: Move to which Hex?**
Infantry attacking **at Range 2-3 after Moving**	-1	1. Within Range & LoS of enemy
Infantry attacking **at Range 2-3 whilst in Square formation**	-1	2. Trees > Buildings hex
Infantry attacking Infantry **who are in Square formation**	+1	3. High Ground hex
Cavalry attacking Infantry **who are in Square formation**	-3	4. Hex not in a River
Artillery attacking **at Range 1-3**	+2	5. Hex Furthest Up
Artillery attacking Infantry **who are in Square formation**	+2	6. Nearest to Corunna
Any unit attacking **which is adjacent to its Commander**	+1	**TB2: Attack which Enemy?**
Any unit attacking **from Higher Ground than its Target**	+1	1. Unit nearest British Commander
Any unit attacking **a unit in Trees or Buildings**	-1	2. Unit Furthest Up
Any unit attacking **through intervening Trees**	-1	3. Unit not in Trees/Buildings
Any unit attacking **from a River hex**	-1	4. Strongest Unit

12. The Battle of Corunna, 1809

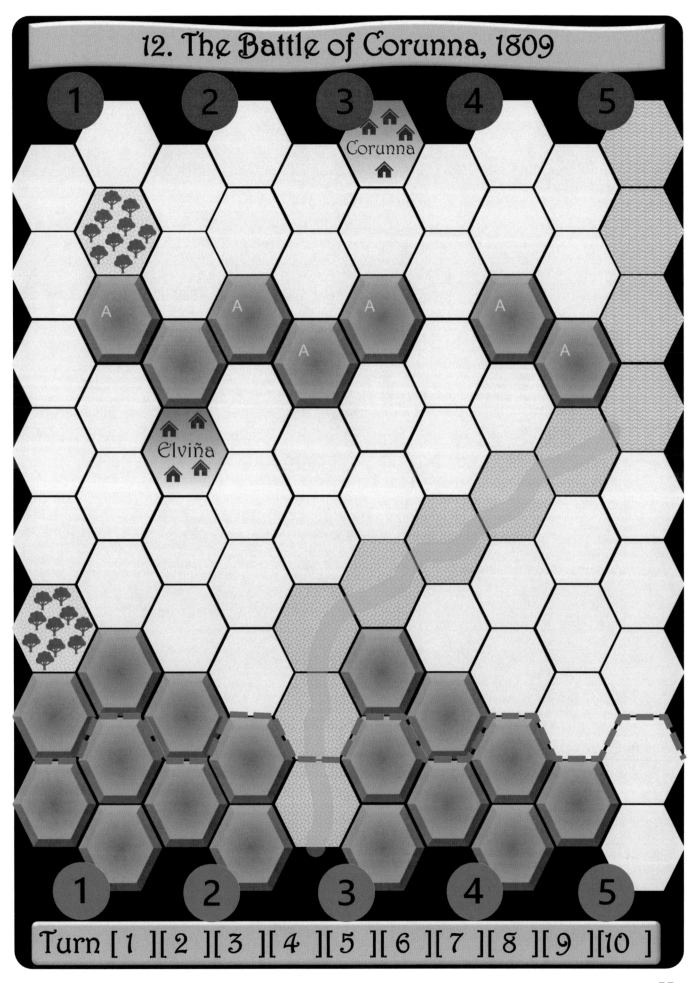

13. The Battle of Talavera, 28 July 1809 (British/German/Spanish)

Having crossed the River Douro, Sir Arthur Wellesley advanced on Madrid where Joseph Bonaparte had been imposed on Spain as King. The French withdrawal gave the British and its allies a narrow victory. **Objective:** *Have more units <u>upwards</u> of the River (not in the River itself) than the French <u>at the end</u> of Turn 10. For both armies, only count units further <u>up</u> the Battle Map than the River.*

Player: British/German/Spanish		Place each Unit below the red dashed line	
Infantry: 5	Cavalry: 2	Artillery: 1	Commander: Sir Arthur Wellesley
Roll **3 dice. Re-roll any dice once** (all together). If Commander **not KIA**, then 6s are Wild			

AI: French	Roll **4 dice. Re-roll all duplicates under 6** (and all **6s** if Comm not KIA) once
Artillery (1)	**Set Up: Roll for Area 1,2,3,4; place on top hex**

	Attack nearest [Ar/Co/In/Cv] [TB2]
4-5	Move horizontally downwards but only to put an enemy unit in Range *and* LoS [TB1]
6	Move straight down, but *not* if that hex is a River hex

Cavalry (2)	**Set Up: Roll for Area; place on fourth hex down**

	Attack Co/In/Ar/Cv [TB2]
2-3	If any enemy is within 3 hexes then select the nearest enemy [upwards of the River] [furthest up]. Move nearer to it [V] [TB1]: Attack In/Cv/Co/Ar [TB2]
4-5	Select nearest enemy [furthest up]. Move nearer to it [V] [TB1]: Attack Co/In/Ar/Cv [TB2]
6	Select nearest enemy [furthest up]. Move nearer to it [H] [TB1]: Attack Co/In/Ar/Cv [TB2]

Infantry (7)	**Set Up: Roll for Area; place on third or, if occupied, second hex down**

If in Square & no enemy Cavalry within 3 hexes then De-Square: Attack nearest [Co/Ar/Cv/In] [TB2]
If not in Square & enemy Cavalry are within 3 hexes then Square: Attack nearest [Co/Ar/Cv/In] [TB2]
Attack nearest [Co/In/Cv/Ar] [TB2]

1-2	If not already on a Trees hex, select an *adjacent* vacant Trees hex [furthest up] [TB1]. Move onto it: Attack nearest [Cv/In/Co/Ar] [TB2]
3-4	Move straight down: Attack nearest [Co/Ar/Cv/In] [TB2]
5-6	Select nearest enemy [furthest up]. Move nearer to it [H] [TB1]: Attack nearest [Co/Ar/Cv/In] [TB2]

Commander: Marshal Soult	**Set Up: Roll for Area 2,3,4; place on second hex down or, if occupied, top hex**

Attack In/Cv/Co/Ar [TB2]
Select a vacant adjacent hex which is itself adjacent to *more* friendly units than the Commander is now [most friendly units] [furthest up] [TB1]. Move into it: Attack In/Cv/Co/Ar [TB2]
Select the nearest *friendly* unit [In/Cv/Ar] [furthest up] [TB1]. Move nearer to it [H] [TB1]: Attack In/Cv/Co/Ar [TB2]

Unit	M	R	Units cannot Move if Square/engaged in battle	v Inf	v Cav	v Art
Infantry	1	3	Move or Square/De-Square, then Attack	4 - 3 - 2	3 - 2 - 2	3 - 2 - 2
Cavalry	2	1	Move, then Attack	6 - 5 - 4	4 - 3 - 2	4 - 3 - 2
Artillery	1	6	Move or Attack	3 - 2	2 - 1	2 - 1

Situation or Terrain (Units, High Ground & Buildings block LoS)	Dice	AI Tiebreaker Rules
Infantry attacking at *Range 1* after Moving	+1	**TB1: Move to which Hex?**
Infantry attacking at *Range 2-3* after Moving	-1	1. Within Range & LoS of enemy
Infantry attacking at *Range 2-3* whilst in Square formation	-1	2. Trees > Buildings hex
Infantry attacking Infantry who are in Square formation	+1	3. High Ground hex
Cavalry attacking Infantry who are in Square formation	-3	4. Hex not in a River
Artillery attacking at Range 1-3	+2	5. Hex Furthest Up
Artillery attacking Infantry who are in Square formation	+2	6. In/nearest to Area 3
Any unit attacking which is adjacent to its Commander	+1	**TB2: Attack which Enemy?**
Any unit attacking from Higher Ground than its Target	+1	1. Unit upwards of the River
Any unit attacking a unit in Trees or Buildings	-1	2. Unit Furthest Up
Any unit attacking through intervening Trees	-1	3. Unit not in Trees/Buildings
Any unit attacking from a River hex	-1	4. Strongest Unit

13. The Battle of Talavera, 1809

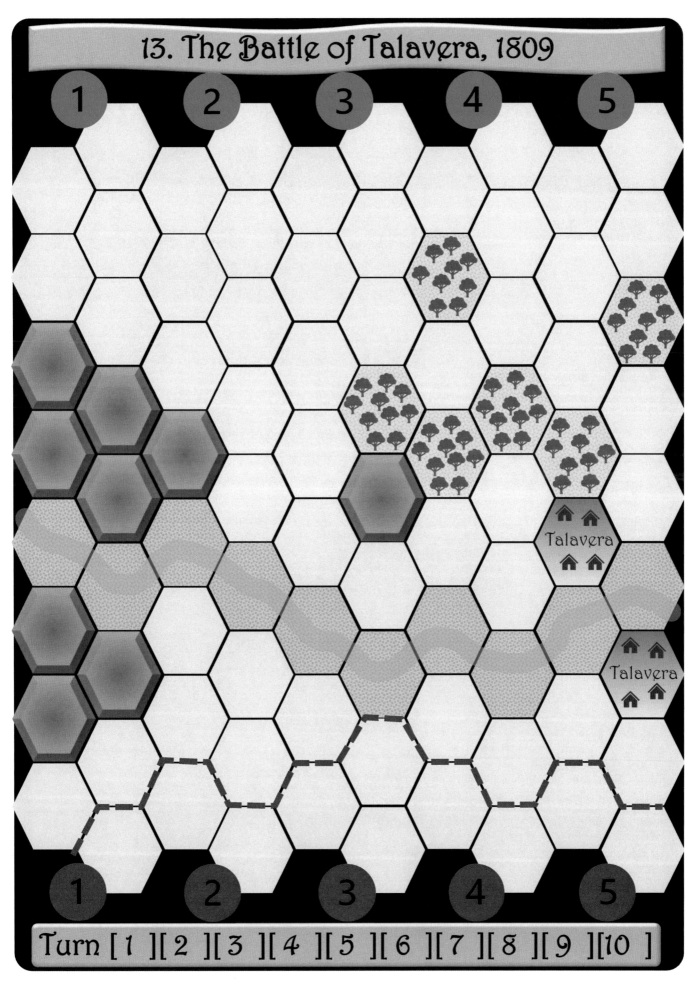

Turn [1][2][3][4][5][6][7][8][9][10]

14. The Battle of Talavera, 28 July 1809 (French)

The same Battle again but from the French point of view. Stop the British advance.

Objective: *Prevent any British unit Moving across the River at any point in the Battle. A unit in the River is not deemed to have crossed it – it must Move to a hex downwards of the River.*

Player: French	Place each Unit below the blue dashed line		
Infantry: 4	Cavalry: 2	Artillery: 1	Commander: Marshal Soult
Roll 3 dice. **Re-roll any dice once** (all together). **If Commander not KIA, then 6s are Wild**			

AI: Brit/German/Spain	Roll 4 dice. Re-roll all duplicates under 6 (and all 6s if Comm not KIA) once
Artillery (1)	**Set Up: Roll for Area 2,3,4; place on second hex down**

Attack nearest [Ar/Co/In/Cv] [TB2]

1-3	Move horizontally downwards but only to put an enemy unit in Range *and* LoS [TB1]
4-6	Move straight down

Cavalry (3)	**Set Up: Roll for Area; place on third hex down**

If it is possible to reach a vacant hex downwards of the River then Move into that hex. If not, ignore this instruction

Attack In/Co/Ar/Cv [TB2]

If **T > 6** Move straight down: Attack In/Cv/Co/Ar [TB2]

1-2	If any enemy is within 3 hexes then select the nearest enemy [furthest up]. Move nearer to it [V] [TB1]: Attack In/Cv/Co/Ar [TB2]
3-4	Select nearest enemy [furthest up]. Move nearer to it [V] [TB1]: Attack Co/In/Ar/Cv [TB2]
5-6	Move straight down: Attack Co/In/Ar/Cv [TB2]

Infantry (6)	**Set Up: Roll for Area; place on fourth or, if occupied, third hex down**

If any vacant adjacent hex is downwards of the River, Move into that hex

Attack nearest [Co/In/Cv/Ar] [TB2]

1-3	Select nearest enemy [furthest up]. Move nearer to it [V][TB1]: Attack nearest [In/Co/Ar/Cv] [TB2]
4-6	Move straight down: Attack nearest [Co/Ar/Cv/In] [TB2]

Commander: Sir Arthur Wellesley	**Set Up: Roll for Area 2,3,4; Place on top hex**

Attack In/Cv/Co/Ar [TB2]

If **T > 7** Move straight down: Attack In/Cv/Co/Ar [TB2]

Select a vacant adjacent hex which is itself adjacent to *more* friendly units than the Commander is now [most friendly units] [furthest up] [TB1]. Move into it: Attack In/Cv/Co/Ar [TB2]

Select nearest *friendly* unit [In/Cv/Ar] [furthest up]. Move nearer to it [H] [TB1]: Attack In/Cv/Co/Ar [TB2]

Unit	M	R	Units cannot Move if Square/engaged in battle	v Inf	v Cav	v Art
Infantry	1	3	Move or Square/De-Square, then Attack	4 - 3 - 2	3 - 2 - 2	3 - 2 - 2
Cavalry	2	1	Move, then Attack	6 - 5 - 4	4 - 3 - 2	4 - 3 - 2
Artillery	1	6	Move or Attack	3 - 2	2 - 1	2 - 1

Situation or Terrain (Units, High Ground & Buildings block LoS)	Dice	AI Tiebreaker Rules	
Infantry attacking **at *Range 1* after Moving**	+1	**TB1: Move to which Hex?**	
Infantry attacking ***at Range 2-3* after Moving**	-1	1. Within Range & LoS of enemy	
Infantry attacking ***at Range 2-3* whilst in Square formation**	-1	2. Trees > Buildings hex	
Infantry attacking Infantry **who are in Square formation**	+1	3. High Ground hex	
Cavalry attacking Infantry **who are in Square formation**	-3	4. Hex not in a River	
Artillery attacking **at Range 1-3**	+2	5. Hex Furthest Down	
Artillery attacking Infantry **who are in Square formation**	+2	6. In/nearest to Area 3	
Any unit attacking **which is adjacent to its Commander**	+1	**TB2: Attack which Enemy?**	
Any unit attacking **from Higher Ground than its Target**	+1	1. Unit Furthest Up	
Any unit attacking **a unit in Trees or Buildings**	-1	2. Unit not in Trees/Buildings	
Any unit attacking **through intervening Trees**	-1	3. Strongest Unit	
Any unit attacking **from a River hex**	-1	4. Unit nearest to Area 3	

14. The Battle of Talavera, 1809

Turn [1][2][3][4][5][6][7][8][9][10]

15. The Battle of Barrosa, 5 March 1811 (British/Portuguese/Spanish)

The British, Portuguese and Spanish armies were marching past Barrosa Hill (Cerro de Porco) when they became embroiled in Battle.

Objective: *Occupy the darker high ground hex (the "Objective") with any unit at the end of Turn 10*

Player: British/Portuguese/Spain		Place each Unit below the red dashed line	
Infantry: 4	Cavalry: 1	Artillery: 1	Commander: Lieutenant General Thomas Graham
Roll 3 dice. **Re-roll any dice once** (all together). **If Commander not KIA**, then 6s are Wild			

AI: French	Roll **4 dice**. **Re-roll all duplicates under 6** (and all **6s if Comm not KIA**) once
Artillery (1)	**Set Up: Roll for Area 1,2; place on top hex**

Attack nearest [Ar/Co/In/Cv] [TB2]

3-4	Move horizontally downwards to the right
5-6	Move straight down

Cavalry (2) Set Up: Roll for Area 1,2,5; place on fourth hex down if Area 1 or 2, third hex down if Area 5

Attack Co/In/Ar/Cv [TB2]

If **T > 7** Move towards Objective [V] [TB1]: Attack Co/Ar/In/Cv [TB2]

1	If any enemy is within 3 hexes then select the nearest enemy [nearest to Objective] [furthest up]. Move nearer to it [V] [TB1]: Attack In/Cv/Co/Ar [TB2]
2-3	Move straight down: Attack Co/In/Ar/Cv [TB2]
4-6	Select nearest enemy [furthest up]. Move nearer to it [V] [TB1]: Attack Co/In/Ar/Cv [TB2]

Infantry (6)   Set Up: Roll for Area 2,3,4,5; place on third or, if occupied, second hex down

If **T > 7** Move towards Objective [H] [TB1]: Attack nearest [Co/Ar/In/Cv] [TB2]

Attack nearest [Co/In/Cv/Ar] [TB2]

1-2	If Objective hex is vacant Move nearer to it [V] [TB1]: Attack nearest [Co/Ar/Cv/In] [TB2]
3-4	Move straight down: Attack nearest [Co/Ar/Cv/In] [TB2]
5-6	Select nearest enemy [furthest up]. Move nearer to it [H] [TB1]: Attack nearest [Co/Ar/Cv/In] [TB2]

Commander: Marshal Victor Set Up: Roll for Area 3,4,5; place on second hex down or, if occupied, top hex

Attack In/Cv/Co/Ar [TB2]

Select a vacant adjacent hex which is itself adjacent to *more* friendly units than the Commander is now [most friendly units] [furthest up] [TB1]. Move into it: Attack In/Cv/Co/Ar [TB2]

Select the nearest *friendly* unit [In/Cv/Ar] [furthest up]. Move nearer to it [H] [TB1]: Attack In/Cv/Co/Ar [TB2]

Unit	M	R	Units cannot Move if Square/engaged in battle	v Inf	v Cav	v Art
Infantry	1	3	Move or Square/De-Square, then Attack	4 - 3 - 2	3 - 2 - 2	3 - 2 - 2
Cavalry	2	1	Move, then Attack	6 - 5 - 4	4 - 3 - 2	4 - 3 - 2
Artillery	1	6	Move or Attack	3 - 2	2 - 1	2 - 1

Situation or Terrain (Units, High Ground & Buildings block LoS)	Dice	AI Tiebreaker Rules
Infantry attacking **at Range 1 after Moving**	+1	**TB1: Move to which Hex?**
Infantry attacking **at Range 2-3 after Moving**	-1	1. Within Range & LoS of enemy
Infantry attacking **at Range 2-3 whilst in Square formation**	-1	2. Trees > Buildings hex
Infantry attacking Infantry **who are in Square formation**	+1	3. High Ground hex
Cavalry attacking Infantry **who are in Square formation**	-3	4. Hex Furthest Up
Artillery attacking **at Range 1-3**	+2	5. Nearest to Objective hex
Artillery attacking Infantry **who are in Square formation**	+2	6. In/nearest to Area 3
Any unit attacking **which is adjacent to its Commander**	+1	**TB2: Attack which Enemy?**
Any unit attacking **from Higher Ground than its Target**	+1	1. Unit nearest Objective hex
Any unit attacking **a unit in Trees or Buildings**	-1	2. Unit Furthest Up
Any unit attacking **through intervening Trees**	-1	3. Unit not in Trees/Buildings
Any unit attacking **from a River hex**	-1	4. Strongest Unit

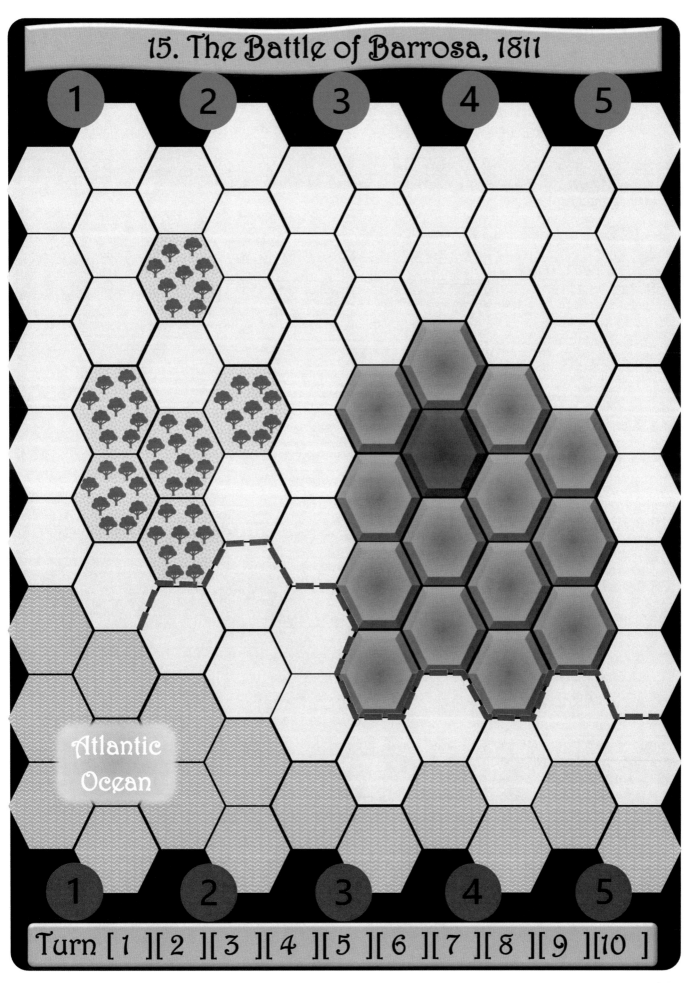

Atlantic Ocean

Turn [1][2][3][4][5][6][7][8][9][10]

16. The Battle of Barrosa, 5 March 1811 (French)

The same Battle again but from the French point of view. Try to dislodge the British from the hill.

Objective: *Have no British unit on the hill (High Ground hex) <u>at the end</u> of Turn 10.*

Player: French	Place each Unit below the blue dashed line		
Infantry: 5	Cavalry: 1	Artillery: 1	Commander: Marshal Victor
Roll 3 dice. **Re-roll any dice once** (all together). If Commander **not KIA**, then 6s are Wild			

AI: Brit/Port/Spanish	Roll 4 dice. **Re-roll all duplicates under 6** (and all **6s** if Comm not KIA) once
Artillery (1) Set Up: Roll for Area 3,5; place on third hex down if Area 3, sixth hex down if Area 5	
Attack nearest [Co/In/Cv/Ar] [TB2]	

4	Move horizontally downwards but only to put an enemy unit in Range *and* LoS [TB1]
5-6	Move straight down, but *not* if the destination hex is a Trees hex

Cavalry (2)	Set Up: Place on fourth hex down of Area 1 and seventh hex down of Area 5
Attack In/Co/Ar/Cv [TB2]	
If **T>7** and unit is not on a High Ground hex, then select nearest High Ground hex [furthest up] [nearest to enemy unit]. Move nearer to it [TB1]: Attack In/Co/Ar/Cv [TB2]	

1-2	If any enemy is within 3 hexes then select the nearest enemy [furthest up]. Move nearer to it [V] [TB1]: Attack In/Cv/Co/Ar [TB2]
3-4	Move straight down: Attack Co/In/Ar/Cv [TB2]
5-6	Select nearest enemy [furthest up]. Move nearer to it [V] [TB1]: Attack Co/In/Ar/Cv [TB2]

Infantry (6) Set Up: Place on each remaining hex which is *adjacent* to the Ocean *except* the hex marked 'C'	
If **T>6** and unit is not on a High Ground hex, then select nearest High Ground hex [furthest up] [nearest to enemy unit]. Move nearer to it [TB1]: Attack nearest [In/Co/Cv/Ar] [TB2]	
Attack nearest [Co/In/Cv/Ar] [TB2]	

4-5	Move straight down, but not if the unit will Move *from* a High Ground hex *to* a low hex: Attack nearest [Co/In/Cv/Ar] [TB2]
6	Select nearest enemy [furthest up]. Move nearer to it [V][TB1]: Attack nearest [Co/Ar/Cv/In] [TB2]

Commander: Lieutenant General Thomas Graham	Set Up: Place on the hex marked 'C'
Attack In/Cv/Co/Ar [TB2]	
If **T>7** and unit is not on a High Ground hex, then select nearest High Ground hex [furthest up] [nearest to enemy unit]. Move nearer to it [TB1]: Attack In/Co/Ar/Cv [TB2]	
Select a vacant adjacent hex which is itself adjacent to *more* friendly units than the Commander is now [most friendly units] [furthest up] [TB1]. Move into it: Attack In/Cv/Co/Ar [TB2]	

Unit	M	R	Units cannot Move if Square/engaged in battle	v Inf	v Cav	v Art
Infantry	1	3	Move or Square/De-Square, then Attack	4 - 3 - 2	3 - 2 - 2	3 - 2 - 2
Cavalry	2	1	Move, then Attack	6 - 5 - 4	4 - 3 - 2	4 - 3 - 2
Artillery	1	6	Move or Attack	3 - 2	2 - 1	2 - 1

Situation or Terrain (Units, High Ground & Buildings block LoS)	Dice	AI Tiebreaker Rules	
Infantry attacking **at *Range 1* after Moving**	+1	**TB1: Move to which Hex?**	
Infantry attacking ***at Range 2-3* after Moving**	-1	1. Within Range & LoS of enemy	
Infantry attacking ***at Range 2-3* whilst in Square formation**	-1	2. Trees > Buildings hex	
Infantry attacking Infantry **who are in Square formation**	+1	3. High Ground hex	
Cavalry attacking Infantry **who are in Square formation**	-3	4. Hex Furthest Down	
Artillery attacking **at Range 1-3**	+2	5. In/nearest to Area 2	
Artillery attacking Infantry **who are in Square formation**	+2		
Any unit attacking **which is adjacent to its** Commander	+1	**TB2: Attack which Enemy?**	
Any unit attacking **from Higher Ground than its Target**	+1	1. Unit on a High Ground hex	
Any unit attacking **a unit in Trees or Buildings**	-1	2. Unit Furthest Up	
Any unit attacking **through intervening Trees**	-1	3. Unit not in Trees/Buildings	
Any unit attacking **from a River hex**	-1	4. Strongest Unit	

16. The Battle of Barrosa, 1811

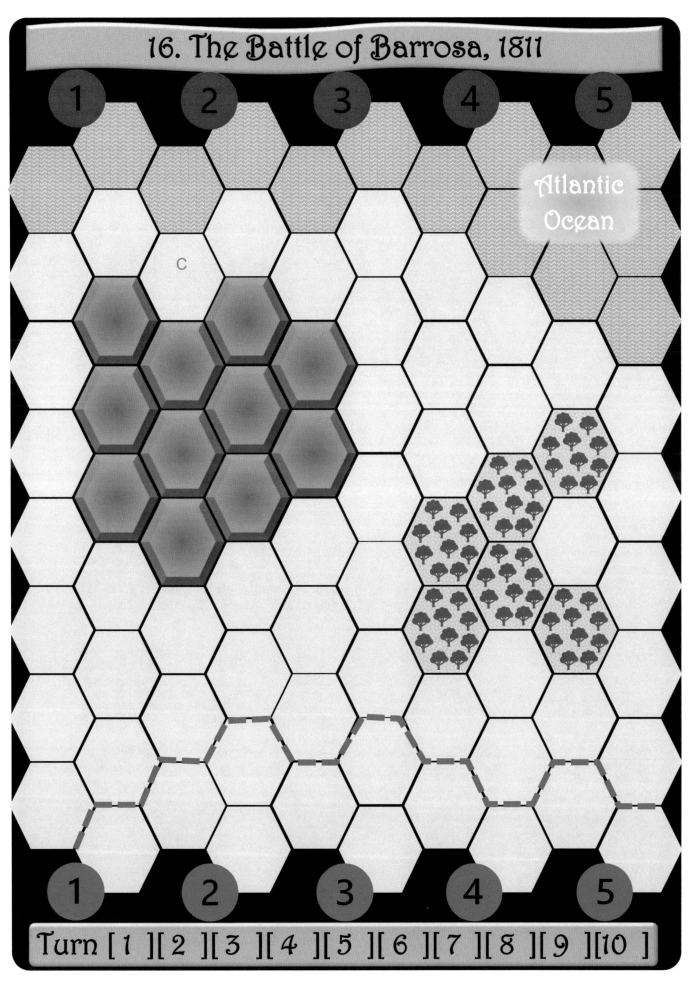

Atlantic Ocean

C

Turn [1][2][3][4][5][6][7][8][9][10]

17. The Battle of Sabugal, 3 April 1811 (British/Portuguese)

Fought in North East Portugal near the Spanish border. Although Wellington's plan to entrap the French did not come off due to appalling weather conditions, the French were forced to retreat.
Objective: *Kill the French Commander.*

Player: British/Portuguese		Place each Unit below the red dashed line	
Infantry: 5	**Cavalry: 2**	**Artillery: 1**	**Commander:** Lieutenant General Viscount Wellington

Roll **3 dice. Re-roll any dice once** (all together). **If Commander not KIA**, then 6s are Wild

AI: French	Roll **4 dice. Re-roll all duplicates under 6** (and all **6s if Comm not KIA**) once
Artillery (1)	**Set Up: Roll for Area 1,2,3; place on second hex down**

Attack nearest [Ar/Co/In/Cv] [TB2]

3	Move horizontally downwards to the right
4-6	Move straight down

Cavalry (1) Set Up:	**Roll for Area 3,4,5; place on top hex**

Attack Co/In/Ar/Cv [TB2]

1	If any enemy is within 3 hexes then select the nearest enemy [furthest up]. Move nearer to it [V] [TB1]: Attack In/Cv/Co/Ar [TB2]
2-4	Move straight down: Attack Co/In/Ar/Cv [TB2]
5-6	Select nearest enemy [furthest up]. Move nearer to it [V] [TB1]: Attack Co/In/Ar/Cv [TB2]

Infantry (7) Set Up: Place on third hex down of each Area and on second hex down of Area 4 & 5

If **T > 5** then Move nearer to the French Commander [V] [TB1]: Attack nearest Cv/Co/In/Ar [TB2]

If in Square & no enemy Cavalry within 3 hexes then De-Square: Attack nearest [Co/Ar/Cv/In] [TB2]

If not in Square & enemy Cavalry are within 3 hexes then Square: Attack nearest [Co/Ar/Cv/In] [TB2]

Attack nearest [Co/In/Cv/Ar] [TB2]

2-4	Move straight down: Attack nearest [Co/Ar/Cv/In] [TB2]
5-6	Select nearest enemy [furthest up]. Move nearer to it [H] [TB1]: Attack nearest [Co/Ar/Cv/In] [TB2]

Commander: Marshal André Massena	**Set Up: Roll for Area 3,4,5; place on top hex**

Attack In/Cv/Co/Ar [TB2]

If **T > 5** Move nearer to hex 'X' [adjacent to most friendly units] [TB1]: Attack In/Cv/Co/Ar [TB2]

If Commander is not directly behind (adjacent to, above *and* in the same column as) a French unit, select a vacant adjacent hex which *is* [furthest up] [TB1]. Move into it: Attack In/Cv/Co/Ar [TB2]

Select nearest *friendly* unit [In/Cv/Ar] [furthest up]. Move nearer to it [H] [TB1]: Attack In/Cv/Co/Ar [TB2]

Unit	M	R	Units cannot Move if Square/engaged in battle	v Inf	v Cav	v Art
Infantry	1	3	Move or Square/De-Square, then Attack	4 - 3 - 2	3 - 2 - 2	3 - 2 - 2
Cavalry	2	1	Move, then Attack	6 - 5 - 4	4 - 3 - 2	4 - 3 - 2
Artillery	1	6	Move or Attack	3 - 2	2 - 1	2 - 1

Situation or Terrain (Units, High Ground & Buildings block LoS)	Dice	AI Tiebreaker Rules
Infantry attacking at *Range 1* after **Moving**	+1	**TB1: Move to which Hex?**
Infantry attacking at *Range 2-3* after **Moving**	-1	1. Within Range & LoS of enemy
Infantry attacking at *Range 2-3* whilst in **Square** formation	-1	2. Trees > Buildings hex
Infantry attacking **Infantry** who are in **Square** formation	+1	3. High Ground hex
Cavalry attacking **Infantry** who are in **Square** formation	-3	4. Hex not in a River
Artillery attacking at **Range 1-3**	+2	5. Hex Furthest Up
Artillery attacking **Infantry** who are in **Square** formation	+2	6. Nearest to French Comm
Any unit attacking **which is adjacent to its Commander**	+1	**TB2: Attack which Enemy?**
Any unit attacking **from Higher Ground than its Target**	+1	1. Unit nearest French Comm
Any unit attacking **a unit in Trees or Buildings**	-1	2. Unit Furthest Up
Any unit attacking **through intervening Trees**	-1	3. Unit not in Trees/Buildings
Any unit attacking **from a River hex**	-1	4. Strongest Unit

17. The Battle of Sabugal, 1811

Sabugal

18. The Battle of Sabugal, 3 April 1811 (French)

The same battle, as the French. Avoid having to retreat by keeping the British and Portuguese back.

Objective: *Have <u>more</u> French units anywhere on the Map than the number of British units that are <u>below</u> the red dashed line, <u>at the end</u> of Turn 10.*

Player: French	Place each Unit below the blue dashed line		
Infantry: 5	Cavalry: 1	Artillery: 1	Commander: Marshal André Massena
Roll **3 dice. Re-roll any dice once** (all together). **If Commander not KIA, then 6s are Wild**			

AI: British/Portuguese	Roll **4 dice. Re-roll all duplicates under 6** (and all **6s if Comm not KIA**) once
Artillery (1)	**Set Up: Roll for Area; place on top hex**

Attack nearest [Ar/Co/In/Cv] [TB2]

1-3	Move horizontally downwards but only to put an enemy unit in Range *and* LoS [TB1]
4-6	Move straight down

Cavalry (3)	**Set Up: Roll for Area; place on fourth hex down**

Attack In/Co/Ar/Cv [TB2]

If **T > 7** and Cavalry unit is above the red dashed line, Move straight down: Attack In/Cv/Co/Ar [TB2]

1-2	If any enemy is within 3 hexes then select the nearest enemy [weakest] [furthest up]. Move nearer to it [V] [TB1]: Attack In/Cv/Co/Ar [TB2]
3-4	Select nearest enemy [furthest up]. Move nearer to it [V] [TB1]: Attack Co/In/Ar/Cv [TB2]
5-6	Move straight down: Attack Co/In/Ar/Cv [TB2]

Infantry (7)	**Set Up: Roll for Area; place on third or, if occupied, second hex down**

Attack nearest [Co/In/Cv/Ar] [TB2]

1	If *below* the red dashed line and not in a Trees hex, select an *adjacent* vacant Trees hex [furthest up]. Move into it: Attack nearest [In/Co/Ar/Cv] [TB2]
2-3	Select nearest enemy [furthest down]. Move nearer to it [V][TB1]: Attack nearest [In/Co/Ar/Cv] [TB2]
4-6	Move straight down: Attack nearest [Co/Ar/Cv/In] [TB2]

Commander: Lieutenant General Viscount Wellington	**Set Up: Roll for Area 2,3,4; Place on top hex**

Attack In/Cv/Co/Ar [TB2]

If **T > 8** and Commander is above the red dashed line, Move straight down: Attack In/Cv/Co/Ar [TB2]

Select a vacant adjacent hex which is itself adjacent to *more* friendly units than the Commander is now [most friendly units] [furthest up] [TB1]. Move into it: Attack In/Cv/Co/Ar [TB2]

Select nearest *friendly* unit [In/Cv/Ar] [furthest up]. Move nearer to it [H] [TB1]: Attack In/Cv/Co/Ar [TB2]

Unit	M	R	Units cannot Move if Square/engaged in battle	v Inf	v Cav	v Art
Infantry	1	3	Move or Square/De-Square, then Attack	4 - 3 - 2	3 - 2 - 2	3 - 2 - 2
Cavalry	2	1	Move, then Attack	6 - 5 - 4	4 - 3 - 2	4 - 3 - 2
Artillery	1	6	Move or Attack	3 - 2	2 - 1	2 - 1

Situation or Terrain (Units, High Ground & Buildings block LoS)	Dice	AI Tiebreaker Rules	
Infantry attacking **at *Range 1* after Moving**	+1	**TB1: Move to which Hex?**	
Infantry attacking **at *Range 2-3* after Moving**	-1	1. Within Range & LoS of enemy	
Infantry attacking **at *Range 2-3* whilst in Square formation**	-1	2. Trees > Buildings hex	
Infantry attacking Infantry **who are in Square formation**	+1	3. High Ground hex	
Cavalry attacking Infantry **who are in Square formation**	-3	4. Hex not in a River	
Artillery attacking **at Range 1-3**	+2	5. Hex Furthest Down	
Artillery attacking Infantry **who are in Square formation**	+2	6. In/nearest to Area 3	
Any unit attacking **which is adjacent to its Commander**	+1	**TB2: Attack which Enemy?**	
Any unit attacking **from Higher Ground than its Target**	+1	1. Unit Furthest Up	
Any unit attacking **a unit in Trees or Buildings**	-1	2. Unit not in Trees/Buildings	
Any unit attacking **through intervening Trees**	-1	3. Weakest Unit	
Any unit attacking **from a River hex**	-1	4. Unit nearest to Area 3	

18. The Battle of Sabugal, 1811

A hard fought Battle in which Wellington prevented Massena from reaching Almeida. **Objective:**
*Occupy the towns of **Fuentes de Oñoro** <u>and</u> **Poco Velho** with any unit <u>at the end</u> of Turn 10.*

Player: British & Portuguese		Place each Unit below the red dashed line	
Infantry: 6	Cavalry: 1	Artillery: 1	Commander: Lieutenant General Viscount Wellington

Roll 3 dice. **Re-roll any dice once** (all together). **If Commander not KIA, then 6s are Wild**

AI: French	Roll **4** dice. **Re-roll all duplicates under 6** (and all **6s** if Comm not KIA) once

Artillery (1)	Set Up: Roll for Area; place on top hex

Attack nearest [Ar/Co/In/Cv] [TB2]

3-4	Move straight down
5-6	Move horizontally downwards but only to put an enemy unit in Range *and* LoS [TB1]

Cavalry (2)	Set Up: Roll for Area 1,2,4,5; place on fourth hex down

Attack Co/In/Ar/Cv [TB2]

1-2	If any enemy is within 3 hexes then select the nearest enemy [nearest to a Buildings hex] [furthest up]. Move nearer to it [V] [TB1]: Attack In/Cv/Co/Ar [TB2]
3-4	Select nearest enemy [furthest up]. Move nearer to it [V] [TB1]: Attack Co/In/Ar/Cv [TB2]
5-6	If **T > 5** select the nearest Buildings hex [Fuentes]. Move nearer to it [V] [TB1]: Attack Co/In/Ar/Cv [TB2]

Infantry (8) Set Up: Place on third hex down of each Area and second hex down of Areas 2,3,4

If in Square & no enemy Cavalry within 3 hexes then De-Square: Attack nearest [Co/Ar/Cv/In] [TB2]

If *on* a Buildings hex and not in Square and enemy Cavalry are within 3 hexes then Square: Attack nearest [Co/Ar/Cv/In] [TB2]

Attack nearest [Co/In/Cv/Ar] [TB2]

1-2	Select the nearest Buildings hex [Fuentes]. Move nearer to it [H] [TB1]: Attack nearest [Co/Ar/Cv/In] [TB2]
3-4	Move straight down: Attack nearest [Co/Ar/Cv/In] [TB2]
5-6	Select nearest enemy [furthest up]. Move nearer to it [V] [TB1]: Attack nearest [Co/Ar/Cv/In] [TB2]

Commander: Marshal André Massena	Set Up: Roll for Area 2,3,4; place on top hex

Attack In/Cv/Co/Ar [TB2]

If **T > 7** select nearest Buildings hex [Fuentes]. Move nearer to it [H] [TB1]: Attack In/Cv/Co/Ar [TB2]

Select a vacant adjacent hex which is itself adjacent to *more* friendly units than the Commander is now [most friendly units] [furthest up] [TB1]. Move into it: Attack In/Cv/Co/Ar [TB2]

Unit	M	R	Units cannot Move if Square/engaged in battle	v Inf	v Cav	v Art
Infantry	1	3	Move or Square/De-Square, then Attack	4 - 3 - 2	3 - 2 - 2	3 - 2 - 2
Cavalry	2	1	Move, then Attack	6 - 5 - 4	4 - 3 - 2	4 - 3 - 2
Artillery	1	6	Move or Attack	3 - 2	2 - 1	2 - 1

Situation or Terrain (Units, High Ground & Buildings block LoS)	Dice	AI Tiebreaker Rules	
Infantry attacking *at Range 1* after Moving	+1	**TB1: Move to which Hex?**	
Infantry attacking *at Range 2-3* after Moving	-1	1. Within Range & LoS of enemy	
Infantry attacking *at Range 2-3* whilst in Square formation	-1	2. Trees > Buildings hex	
Infantry attacking Infantry who are in Square formation	+1	3. High Ground hex	
Cavalry attacking Infantry who are in Square formation	-3	4. Hex not in a River	
Artillery attacking *at Range 1-3*	+2	5. Hex Furthest Up	
Artillery attacking Infantry who are in Square formation	+2	6. Nearest to a Buildings hex	
Any unit attacking which is adjacent to its Commander	+1	**TB2: Attack which Enemy?**	
Any unit attacking from Higher Ground than its Target	+1	1. Unit nearest to Buildings hex	
Any unit attacking a unit in Trees or Buildings	-1	2. Unit Furthest Up	
Any unit attacking through intervening Trees	-1	3. Unit not in Trees/Buildings	
Any unit attacking from a River hex	-1	4. Strongest Unit	

19. The Battle of Fuentes de Oñoro, 1811

Fuentes de Oñoro

Poco Velho

20. The Battle of Fuentes de Oñoro, 3 May 1811 (French)

As the French, try to reach Almeida.

Objective: *Move the French Commander,* Marshal Massena, *into Almeida at any point in the Battle.*

Player: French	Place each Unit below the blue dashed line		
Infantry: 4	Cavalry: 2	Artillery: 1	Commander: Marshal André Massena
Roll 3 dice. **Re-roll any dice once** (all together). If Commander **not KIA**, then 6s are Wild			

AI: British/Portuguese	Roll 4 dice. **Re-roll all duplicates under 6** (and all **6s** if Comm not KIA) once
Artillery (1)	**Set Up: Roll for Area 1,2; place on second hex down**

Attack nearest [Co/In/Cv/Ar] [TB2]	
3-4	Move horizontally downwards to the right
5-6	Move straight down, but *not* if the destination hex is a River hex

Cavalry (2)	**Set Up: Place on fourth hex down of Areas 4 & 5**

Attack Co/In/Ar/Cv [TB2]	
1-3	If any enemy is within 3 hexes then select the nearest enemy [strongest] [furthest up]. Move nearer to it [V] [TB1]: Attack Co/In/Cv/Ar [TB2]
4-5	Select nearest enemy [furthest up] [nearest to Almeida]. Move nearer to it [V] [TB1]: Attack Co/In/Ar/Cv [TB2]
6	Move towards French Commander [V] [TB1]: Attack Co/In/Ar/Cv [TB2]

Infantry (7)	**Set Up: Place on third hex down of each Area and second hex down of Areas 3,4**

Attack nearest [Co/In/Cv/Ar] [TB2]	
If T > 6 Move towards Almeida [H] [TB1]. Attack nearest [Co/In/Cv/Ar] [TB2]	
1-2	Move towards Almeida [H] [TB1]. Attack nearest [Co/In/Cv/Ar] [TB2]
3	Select an *adjacent* vacant High Ground hex [furthest down] [nearest to Almeida]. Move into it: Attack nearest [Co/In/Ar/Cv] [TB2]
4	Move towards the French Commander [H] [Furthest down] [TB1]: Attack Co/In/Cv/Ar [TB2]
5-6	Select nearest enemy [furthest up] [nearest to Almeida]. Move nearer to it [V][TB1]: Attack nearest [Co/In/Ar/Cv] [TB2]

Commander: Lieutenant General Viscount Wellington	**Roll for Area 3,4,5; Place on top hex**

Attack Co/In/Cv/Ar [TB2]
If T>7 Move towards French Commander [H] [Furthest up] [TB1]: Attack Co/In/Cv/Ar [TB2]
Select a vacant adjacent hex which is itself adjacent to *more* friendly units than the Commander is now [most friendly units] [furthest up] [TB1]. Move into it: Attack Co/In/Cv/Ar [TB2]
Select nearest *friendly* unit [In/Cv/Ar] [furthest up]. Move nearer to it [H] [TB1]: Attack Co/In/Cv/Ar [TB2]

Unit	M	R	Units cannot Move if Square/engaged in battle	v Inf	v Cav	v Art
Infantry	1	3	Move or Square/De-Square, then Attack	4 - 3 - 2	3 - 2 - 2	3 - 2 - 2
Cavalry	2	1	Move, then Attack	6 - 5 - 4	4 - 3 - 2	4 - 3 - 2
Artillery	1	6	Move or Attack	3 - 2	2 - 1	2 - 1

Situation or Terrain (Units, High Ground & Buildings block LoS)	Dice	AI Tiebreaker Rules	
Infantry attacking **at *Range 1* after Moving**	+1	**TB1: Move to which Hex?**	
Infantry attacking ***at Range 2-3* after Moving**	-1	1. Within Range & LoS of enemy	
Infantry attacking ***at Range 2-3* whilst in Square formation**	-1	2. Trees > Buildings hex	
Infantry attacking Infantry **who are in Square formation**	+1	3. High Ground hex	
Cavalry attacking Infantry **who are in Square formation**	-3	4. Hex not in a River	
Artillery attacking **at Range 1-3**	+2	5. Hex Furthest Up	
Artillery attacking Infantry **who are in Square formation**	+2	6. Nearest to Almeida	
Any unit attacking **which is adjacent to its Commander**	+1	**TB2: Attack which Enemy?**	
Any unit attacking **from Higher Ground than its Target**	+1	1. Unit Furthest Up	
Any unit attacking **a unit in Trees or Buildings**	-1	2. Unit not in Trees/Buildings	
Any unit attacking **through intervening Trees**	-1	3. Strongest Unit	
Any unit attacking **from a River hex**	-1	4. Nearest to Almeida	

20. The Battle of Fuentes de Oñoro, 1811

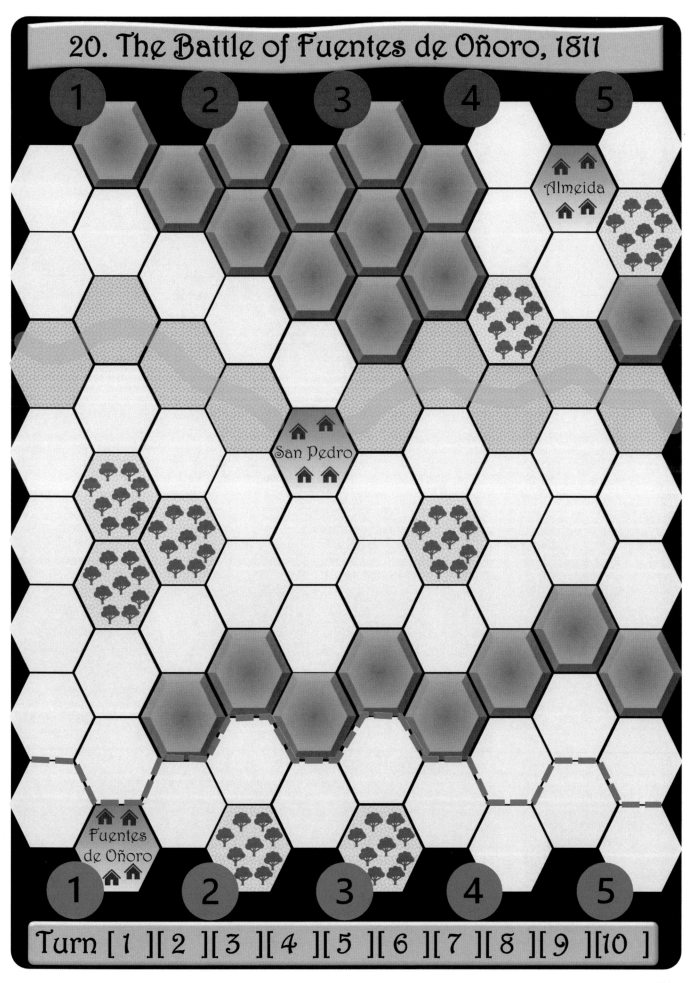

Turn [1][2][3][4][5][6][7][8][9][10]

Suggested Counters

Whilst not necessary, some Players might like to copy or remove this page and stick these counters onto medium card with a very thin layer of PVA glue or similar, in order to use them on the various maps. Cut them up carefully with good quality scissors or a craft knife once the glue is completely dry. Seek adult supervision if necessary.

You can see me make counters for my games on my **YouTube** channel:

Mike Lambo Solitaire Book Games

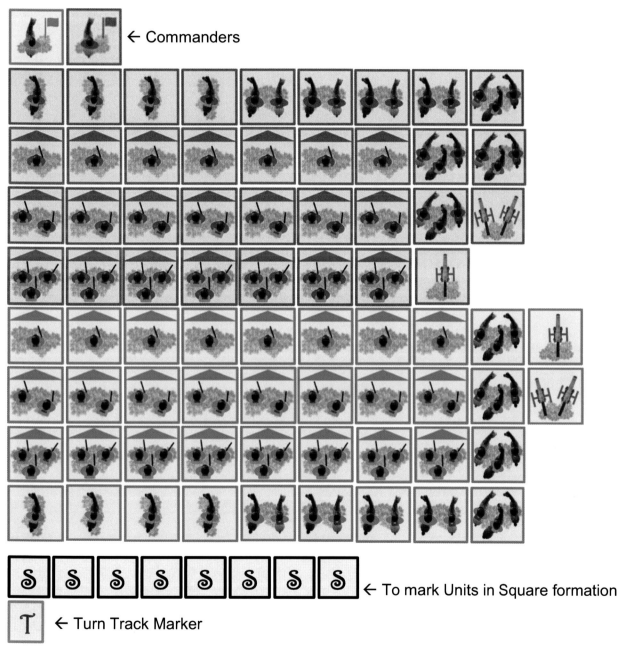

← Commanders

← To mark Units in Square formation

← Turn Track Marker

A copy of this page will also be placed in the *Files* section of the "Battles of Napoleonic Europe" game page on www.BoardGameGeek.com